*Fun is good.*
~DR. SEUSS

# CONTENTS

# CONTENTS

# FOREWORD

## by Chris Brady

When it comes to equipping oneself for leadership and success, many words come to mind: vision, goals, execution, teamwork, metrics, mentors, knowledge, perseverance, and others. However, one particular word that is critical not only to success but to the very enjoyment of it is often overlooked and usually downright ignored. That word is *fun*.

The concept of fun doesn't get much focus. If anything, it is seen as a mere by-product of success, or perhaps one of the facets of success that makes all the hard work of earning it worthwhile. But as this little book will show you, fun is much more than the result of success; it is actually one of its most effective enablers.

Ultimately, nobody succeeds alone. Success is always with, through, and for other people. And people, though each individually unique, are alike in a lot of important ways. One of the most common threads running through the human experience is the desire to enjoy the journey. Strangely, however, although this desire is universal, the fulfillment of it is alarmingly rare. Although everyone enjoys a good laugh, laughter is seldom heard. Although everyone enjoys the bonding of good times shared, good times are scarcer than we'd like. And although everyone aches for joy, joy is largely missing. Therein lies the opportunity to utilize fun to great ends.

Leaders face all sorts of opposition on their quest for success and significance. Among these is the difficulty of enlisting other people to the cause, especially for the long haul. Financial incentives often fail to motivate, recognition is fleeting, and a sense of accomplishment can be only too distant over the extended course of a project. But the leader that can manage to make it fun along the way stands to accomplish more than he or she could with all the other motivators combined.

Think of the times when you've really felt rewarded in your work. If you examine the elements of why those moments were so fulfilling, you'll likely notice that there was a challenge, the work was interesting, and you made reasonable progress. But usually you'll find that there was an element of fun involved, too. There was laughter, camaraderie with coworkers, and an empowering sense of achievement. These conditions almost never exist in an environment of drudgery. Usually, all these elements of meaningful contribution are wrapped in an aura of fun. They were fun because they were fun, and the fact that they were fun made them fun!

What?

Fun is a circular concept! When we are engaged in meaningful activity, we discover that our work can become the most fun fun there is! (That is not a typo. I really meant to say the word *fun* twice!) But we also learn that work can be more meaningful if we strive to intentionally make it fun. In fact, some of the best leaders and highest achievers have discovered this serious power of fun: namely, that fun can make anything more rewarding, more motivating, and more achievable. Fun becomes one of the motivators *as well as* one of the rewards. Very few success factors work on both sides of the equation in just this way.

Fun, though obvious as an idea, is way more important than you may have ever realized. It is a specific implement in the toolbox of a high achiever, wielded to make things both better along the way *and* more worth it at the end.

**Chris Brady**
*New York Times* Bestselling Author
Cofounder, CEO, and Creative Director of LIFE Leadership

# PROLOGUE

*W*e *shut down Steve's drives and Kirk's outside game. Although Aron hit a couple of wing shots, it wasn't enough to keep them in the game. Bill had his best day of the series, scoring at will inside and out.*

*Holger also had his best day, rebounding better than ever and scoring on many offensive rebounds. Finally, my long-range jumper kept the defense spread out, allowing Bill the spacing for his drives.*

*The PC (Policy Council) team won the first game 11–5 and the second one 11–2. The momentum had turned with our best performance to date, and we looked forward to the next day with a three-day to two lead in the series.*

## Thrill of Victory

*Everyone expected Tuesday to be the most intense competition yet as the BoB (Band of Brothers) faced elimination and the PC team focused on ending the series. We knew we had better finish the series before the younger legs wore us down.*

*All weekend long, Holger, Bill, and I contemplated what the BoB would do to slow our aggressive defense and inside/outside juggernaut from the day before. Not surprisingly, when day six started, the answer from the BoB was clear.*

*First, the BoB came an hour early to practice at the Columbiaville elementary school. They worked on various maneuvers to check our game plan, even going as far as setting plays called out by number! The level of competition this day lived up to its advance billing, with neither team giving an inch.*

*In fact, I remember at one point thinking this is exactly what John Wooden had described in his book on competitive greatness. It is simply awesome to experience a game that pushes a person to his competitive limit with other winners doing the same thing!*

## Agony of Defeat

*Nevertheless, only one team could win the series, and the BoB felt it should be them. They blew our doors off in game one. No, they didn't just win; they annihilated us by a score of 11–2!*

*Later, I learned one of their PDCAs (Plan, Do, Check, Adjust) was a realization that the team that had won the first game eventually won the day's contest; therefore, they poured everything into game one for the victory.*

*The BoB played with reckless abandon, letting no shot go unchallenged and owning every loose ball. How could anyone keep up a pace like this?*

*The PC team didn't panic after the blistering defeat but did make some adjustments. Holger promised to step up his rebounding, while Bill committed to take the ball to the rim and pass it back to me if he was double-teamed.*

*Despite our team being exhausted from the physical pounding in game one, I believe the BoB team members were even more spent (as it is practically impossible to play that hard for any sustained length of time). They had truly left it all on the court in game one.*

*Our offense finally started to click, and we came back to return the favor on the exhausted BoB by trouncing them 11–2 in the second game.*

*The whole series pivoted on the final game. Would the PC team pull it off, or would the BoB send the series to day seven?*

## The Joy of Learning

*The whole series now boiled down to one game for the Band of Brothers (BoB). If they lost, it was over; otherwise, with a win, both teams would settle it once and for all on day seven.*

*Each team experienced the increasing pressure and grueling exhaustion of reaching our competitive limit. Nevertheless, it is an athlete's dream to experience true competitive greatness when one's physical limits are reached and mental discipline must take over. What could be more fun? This was epic!*[1]

**Orrin Woodward**
*New York Times* Bestselling Author
Cofounder and Chairman of the Board of LIFE Leadership

INTRODUCTION

# Designed Gratification

*People rarely succeed unless they have
fun in what they are doing.*

~DALE CARNEGIE

You can have more fun in your life. We all can. If you're
on the path of success, in whatever field your particular passions and purpose have set you, you've probably
noticed that there's a lot of hard work involved.

This isn't to say that it's all bad. (You've likely experienced your share of good times and joy throughout the
journey.) But it is usually true that, as Thomas Paine put
it, "Heaven knows how to put a proper price upon its
goods."[1] Success comes after great effort.

So whether you're striving for more prosperity, strength-
ened or healed families, freedom, more happiness, better
relationships, increased world peace, or anything else
truly worth fighting for, you'll pay a fair but hefty price
for it.

**If You Don't Have Fun...**

Understanding this, you should also realize that if you don't have fun in your work, work's no fun. Period. In fact, this principle can be applied to any aspect of life—and even to life itself.

If you don't have fun in your relationships, relationships are no fun.

If you don't have fun at school, school's no fun.

If you don't have fun with your exercise, exercise is no fun.

And most important, if you don't have fun in life, life's no fun.

Let's be clear on one point: Life should be fun—really fun. A good life includes lots of fun. It truly does. Sometimes we forget this, but life is meant to be fun.

> If you don't have fun in life, life's no fun.

Of course it will be hard. Of course it will be challenging. Of course there will be times when you wonder what it's all about. But of course it should be loads of fun! Having fun in life is what makes life fun. And we're not just funning with you.

Let's take it a step further though because this point really matters. You will accomplish far more in life if you learn to enjoy it. That "more" will come in all sorts of ways, both in terms of quality and quantity. You will complete more tasks on your checklist and

> You will accomplish far more in life if you learn to enjoy it.

reach more goals on your bucket list, and each one will mean more because of the energy and effort you put forth to make it a real success.

Not that life is about checking items off lists, but we all have some important goals we ought to accomplish before we die. And doing them excellently is a good start at a successful life.

Naturally, there should be a level of judgment and consideration put into how you prioritize these goals. However, once you know what you should be doing with your time—and which tasks you need to be doing now—you simply need to be accomplishing them. (It's a given that doing them well is always better than doing them poorly or not at all.)

Making these tasks and projects fun—even though they're important, necessary, or urgent—is a great way to keep them happening and growing at an ever-improving rate of success and excellence. And the key to fun is Designed Gratification!

### *Design* Your Gratification

Bestselling author Robert Kiyosaki taught that (along with a long-term vision and an understanding of the power of compounding) understanding and applying the concept of delayed gratification is one of the top three factors that sets highly successful people apart from their less successful counterparts.

While this is absolutely true and an extremely important aspect of success and personal development, we'd like to suggest that the concept of *designed* gratification is another must-have in your path toward leadership and success.

What this means is that being able to delay your gratification in view of your long-term vision isn't the only part of gratification that's vital to your success and happiness.

You also have to learn to design your gratification in small, bite-sized chunks that come all throughout, making the journey fun and endurable. Making your journey *en*durable makes you as a journeyer *durable*.

> Making your journey *endurable* makes you as a journeyer *durable*.

That's what designed gratification is: the stuff that makes the whole adventure fun along the way. Ultimately, if you try to leave the fun part for the very end, you probably won't make it there at all, and if you do, the process won't be very enjoyable. In fact, it will take longer and mean less exactly *because* it wasn't fun.

## Jet Lag, Hotel Pillows, and Business Meetings

Imagine you wake up at 3:00 a.m. You throw your bags in the car, and your spouse drives you to the airport. You wait in line—several different lines, in fact—until everything is checked in and ready. Then you have to wait some more before your plane ever takes off. And *then* you'll have a several-hour series of flights to add to your day's amusements.

When you land, you'll have more lines, stops, and waits to top off the whole exquisite experience—only to deal with jet lag, hotel pillows, and endless business meetings for the week before you head back.

This is arguably an un-fun experience, even if you do your work hopefully and even though you understand that it's all leading up to a phone-free weekend with your spouse in Florida—someday.

In other words, it's time to inject some fun into your life!

## Fun = The Difference

Consider the difference a real understanding of designed gratification and a dedication to having fun in life would make in this experience.

For one, if you're flying with Southwest Airlines, their understanding of the power of fun might be a bright spot in your trip as the flight attendants explain the most boring and simple details of flying guidelines using song, dance, rap, and all sorts of creative, if not bizarre, techniques to make those basic but vital issues seem fun. If you've had this experience, you know how enjoyable it can be.

In fact, this kind of Southwest Airlines approach is a key for life: infuse fun into everything, from the most routine parts of life to the most challenging and also the most exciting.

Add to this your own personal plan for making the whole trip fun, and you could

> Infuse fun into everything, from the most routine parts of life to the most challenging and also the most exciting.

enjoy time on an important project, a couple of great books and audios, and a whole bunch of excellent thinking time.

You won't just get to cross some items off your list. You'll also get to remove "have a totally boring trip" from the list entirely. And who wouldn't want to do that?

It basically comes down to this: If you're going to go through life doing things you've got to do, why not enjoy what you do—especially since it will actually make everything work out that much better?

That said, this book is all about how you can effectively design your gratification to work for you. You'll make your vital behaviors your most exciting and engaging projects and find ways to bring in the simple things that make your life yours. As a result, you'll *have fun* in life, and life will *be fun*!

And let's be clear: Having fun (feeling happy) is good for us. Just consider the following words from famous Harvard teacher Shawn Achor:

> *Happiness can improve our physical health, which in turn keeps us working faster and longer and therefore makes us more likely to succeed....*
>
> *Companies and leaders who take measures to cultivate a happy workplace will not only have more productive and efficient workers—they'll have less absenteeism and lower healthcare expenditures....*
>
> *Every time employees experience a small burst of happiness, they get primed for creativity and innovation. They see solutions they might otherwise have missed.*[2]

In short, happiness and fun in the workplace and in life have a direct influence on our success and progress. And in many cases, happiness can start with genuine fun.

There are countless ways to infuse more fun into your life. And this book will show you how.

We'll share some ideas and stories on how to do this, and by the time you've finished reading the book, you'll have the hang of how to make any and every day a lot more fun. Designed gratification is incredibly powerful because it unleashes the power of fun into our lives.

So buckle up. Take the wheel. And in the words of bestselling author Chris Brady, start "texting from [your] iPhone while driving and eating cereal." Okay, not really. But do get ready—and keep reading—because this is going to be incredibly fun!

# BITE-SIZE FUN

This week's date night, instead of going to a movie or a restaurant, prepare a little picnic and surprise your spouse. (If you haven't done date night in a while, do it now!) A picnic is usually about 1.3 million times more fun than a restaurant (source unknown). If it's winter in your area when you read this book, an indoor picnic by the fireplace will do the trick. Try it; it will make your whole week! The little things are often the most fun.

:)

## CHAPTER ONE

# Laughter

*Life is worth living as long as there's a laugh in it.*

~L. M. MONTGOMERY

S top reading and laugh.

Seriously. Just curl up the ends of your mouth and start laughing. Laugh deeply. Laugh softly. But laugh!

If you're in a public place or a meeting when you read this, do it anyway. Then smile happily at the people who look at you and say, "Isn't this a great day?"

The truth is if you're in the kind of meeting that caused you to start reading a book, everybody there could probably really use a laugh!

Laughter is fun. So laugh. Right now. And don't stop until you've had your fill.

When it comes to fun, laughter is easily the first step because it's the simplest, most basic, and easiest-to-achieve form of good, healthy fun—not to mention the fact that it makes life better in a ton of different ways.

Comedian Victor Borge said, "Laughter is the shortest distance between two people." Laughter truly brings us together in a beautiful and sometimes miraculous way.

It helps us relate to each other, and it helps us trust each other.

Maya Angelou even went so far as to say, "I don't trust anyone who doesn't laugh." While this is perhaps an extreme view, it certainly raises an interesting point: If you can't laugh and have fun with someone, what can you do with that person?

> Laughter truly brings us together in a beautiful and sometimes miraculous way. It helps us relate to each other, and it helps us trust each other.

As many have said over the years, laughing and crying are among the deepest of human expressions, and if your relationship can't allow the good and the happy, there probably isn't enough trust and love to get into the sad and the painful. Yet this type of vulnerability and openness is often crucial to real depth and growth in any relationship.

A group of people who have shared a deep, hysterical, knee-slapping, belly-aching laughing session is a group of people who share a special bond. It's also a group of people who have experienced some serious fun together.

When you get right down to it, that kind of laughing is just plain fun. End of story. Or actually, it's often the beginning of the story—because laughter creates friendships.

So if you value a fun work environment and family dynamic or really any situation that's truly fun (and we're suggesting that you should), creating a culture and atmosphere of appropriate humor and real laughter is a good place to start.

## Start Laughing

So start laughing! As Charles Dickens taught in *A Christmas Carol,* "There is nothing in the world so irresistibly contagious as laughter and good humor." We think this statement, though perhaps not literally accurate, represents a true principle: if you want a group of people to share in fantastic laughing sessions, be the one who makes them happen.

> If you want a group of people to share in fantastic laughing sessions, be the one who makes them happen.

Start laughing yourself, and look for opportunities to help others share in good-natured, lighthearted jokes and fun.

By the way, there is a reason for this that goes beyond fun. Great leaders are frequently great laughers. The two go hand in hand. For example, business leader Orrin Woodward understands this principle, and he frequently uses his personal power to influence and impact the fun level of his team and associates. Here's what he said:

> Start laughing yourself, and look for opportunities to help others share in good-natured, lighthearted jokes and fun.

*Once I was with a group of newer business partners. It was early in our friendship, and we were taking a tour of Staten Island and the Statue of Liberty. Well, we were listening to those audios they have—you know the ones that tell you about everything you're seeing on the tour—and I decided to have some fun.*

*When we came to the next part of the tour, I started talking—saying all kinds of stuff! Some I knew from history, and some was the most random and bizarre stuff I could make up on the spot and make sound believable. The trick of the whole thing was that when people would ask about it, I'd start yelling out random track numbers on the audio where they could find it.*

*They'd all go search and try to find this information, but it wouldn't be there! I even tried skipping around on the audio and adding things they hadn't got to yet on theirs to add to the experience. When they finally realized what was happening, we all had a huge laugh!*

*It was great at breaking the ice for semi-new acquaintances, and it instantly created a memory and camaraderie that's lasted for years and even comes back to cheer us up and make us laugh during difficulties and trials. We'd all start joking that we just needed to know what track to go to, to solve all our problems!*

Imagine how you would feel when the audio started telling you things the guy in your group had already said and when he grinned widely and told you what he'd been doing! Everyone laughed and laughed.

This is the power of laughter. Not only is it one of the universal love languages, but it is one that creates instant bonds between those who share in it as well as powerful and lasting memories that continue to pull them together for years to come. Woodward went on:

> In a very similar scenario with a different group of people at a zoo tour, I found another opportunity to start the laughing.
>
> Every time we'd come to a new exhibit, I'd sneak and read the info sign and learn all about the animal, without anyone noticing. I had to be pretty sneaky and fast, but I was determined.
>
> Once I'd done my quick speed read, I'd station myself strategically between the others and the sign and start pointing out the facts I'd learned about each animal.
>
> Everyone was shocked and amazed at my incredibly specific and intimate knowledge and expertise on every obscure animal we came to at the zoo! They were all asking themselves, "What kind of guy is this, and how does he have time to study so much about all these animals?"
>
> After six or eight such stops, someone spotted me checking out the placard, and I was busted. Uproarious laughter ensued, and it is still a great shared memory for all of us today!

This is how Woodward used humor to build relationships and provide some fun.

Of course, it is important to be smart about when and when not to use humor. Note that in business meetings with the same two groups of people, Orrin knew when to be all about business. In his words, "We take our business very seriously; ourselves, not so much."

> Laughing at the right things at the right times creates immediate and lasting bonds between people.

Laughing at the right things at the right times creates immediate and lasting bonds between people. This is a powerful truth because it means lots of fun right now and all sorts of possibilities for the future.

> "Anything with the power to make you laugh over thirty years later isn't a waste of time."
> ~Stephen King

As Stephen King put it, "Anything with the power to make you laugh over thirty years later isn't a waste of time."[1]

As you create the right kind of laughter in your relationships and interactions, you'll be making your present and future fun deeper, stronger, and better.

### When Life Gives You Lemons, Laugh at That Funny-Looking Fruit!

Another important advantage of laughter that will help you have the kind of fun in life that makes life fun is simply recognizing what aspects of yourself and your experiences are just so funny that they'll either make you laugh or cry. We suggest that it's generally more fun to laugh.

Sometimes this means laughing specifically at yourself; other times, it means laughing at your challenges or even your defeats and failures. In any event, learning to laugh at these low points, to relax and have fun with them, is a great way to make your life more enjoyable and even more effective.

As long as you go from laughing at them to learning from them, this is a great way to spring from failure to failure to failure until you make it to success. And you'll be having a blast as you go.

James Carlos Blake wrote, "A man who can laugh at himself is truly blessed, for he will never lack for amusement." Let's face it, whoever you are, if you learn to laugh at yourself whenever your actions, thoughts, or personal qualities are hilarious, you'll have people on the subway or in the grocery store wondering about the person they hear laughing hysterically.

You're that funny! We all are. So have fun with it. If you're going to be the most entertaining comedian who ever walked or breathed, you may as well enjoy it. We promise it'll be fun.

Of course, we're not saying you should spend *all* your time laughing at yourself and getting weird looks from your fellow shoppers. In fact, we think doing so will hurt your influence in the world greatly and waste a lot of your time.

But what we *are* saying is that you should take a little time and energy in your life and spend it on enjoying the funny things.

It will also benefit you immensely as a leader, mentor, and parent if you help those you lead, teach, or raise learn to laugh at themselves as well. This is quite a legacy to leave them, and it has the power to revolutionize their entire happiness game.

Top leader Chris Brady told the story of how he shared some fun with a good friend and business partner by periodically giving him the opportunity to laugh.

Chris wrote about his friend and accomplished leader: "Claude Hamilton was once very tired on stage and was all slumped down in his chair. I took a picture from the monitor backstage and occasionally send it to him unannounced."

Imagine Claude opening his e-mail in the morning, and there's that picture again!

Of course, before you can go around trying to get people to tease themselves, you have to build your relationship to that level of trust and closeness. But once you do, helping them learn to laugh at themselves, and allowing them to return the favor, can be a lot of fun.

> When people learn to laugh at themselves, they are really learning to love themselves.

When people learn to laugh at themselves, they are really learning to love themselves in the right ways while fully understanding their human flaws and weaknesses.

People who have mastered this are really the happiest ones around because they don't need anyone else to make life fun for them. Learn to laugh at yourself!

# RaNDOM FUN :)

*I'd like to die peacefully in my sleep like my grandfather...not screaming in terror like the passengers on his bus.*
~Jack Handey

*Note to reader: Every once in a while in this book, you'll find a Random Fun box like the one above. It doesn't have much to do with the rest of the book, except that it's just plain fun.*

## Laugh Away Problems

While you're at it, remember that life will send you curveballs other than your own delightful eccentricities. You're going to face challenges, hard times, and even defeats and failure. Apply the same principle to these situations, and really learn to laugh at your lemons as you're making your delicious summertime beverage.

> Learn to laugh at your lemons as you're making your delicious summertime beverage.

Phil Callaway wrote, "In the darkest of times, laughter helps revolutionize our perspective."[2] As you learn to laugh in the face of your most difficult trials and your uttermost failures, you will find yourself better able to pick up the pieces and find the new perspective to launch you upward on your next attempt at flight.

Doing this will make life much better. You will be more effective in your endeavors toward the things that really matter to you, and the entire journey will be that much more fun. Ellen J. Barrier said, "Life is a journey; let's enjoy it, seeing some exciting things, and having fun along the way."

Of course, you're a lot more likely to laugh in difficult times if it's already a habit!

Robert Townsend really added to the discussion when he said, "Getting there isn't half the fun; it's all the fun." So don't waste the journey being sad, angry, bored, or overwhelmed. Have fun. Make it happen. Laugh at yourself. Laugh at your life. Laugh with your friends.

As you do, you'll find there's *plenty* to laugh about!

## Laugh about It All—Forever

Once, when Chris Brady and several associates were on a business trip touring the countryside in rental cars, Chris found himself in what he described as a "painfully slow Suzuki truck."

Somewhere along the way, he took to calling the old thing "Su-suckie." The name made its way through the group, and everyone had several good laughs about it.

By anchoring humor in this shared experience, these good friends created an easy laugh for themselves—one full of fond memories of the old days—anytime they see that brand name.

Fifteen years later, none of them can help but burst out in fits of laughter when they recall that trip with old Su-suckie. Between that and the memories and laughs they continue to create, life stays fun.

In fact, every day can be fun. We just need to look for what's funny all around us. An old saying proclaims: "Live. Laugh. Love." That's great wisdom for a happy and successful life. Have you laughed enough today? If not, start!

## BITE-SIZE FUN

If you have a pet, go play with him or her right now. Tickle your pet, throw a ball, or do whatever he or she likes. Just ten minutes of fun with a pet will put more pep in your whole day. Don't wait. Go now!

CHAPTER TWO

# Competition

*I'll insist my competitor is the greatest,*
*so that when I beat him, I won't be calling myself*
*the greatest—I'll be proving it through my actions.*

~JAROD KINTZ

In the prologue of this book, we introduced you to a
story of intense competition between business partners
and friends. In truth, competition can be a lot of fun.

Psychologist Charles Schaefer said, "We are never more
fully alive, more completely ourselves, or more deeply
engrossed in anything than when we are at play."

This is fairly easy to see in our own lives because we
tend to define the ways we play by the things that engage
us and make us come alive. In a
way, that's what fun is all about:
making us feel completely
engaged in and excited about
what we're doing.

> In a way, fun is all
> about making us feel
> completely engaged
> in and excited about
> what we're doing.

But in our modern world,
this too often is not the case with
our work environment. Work frequently isn't designed

around the things we care about most or the things that are fun to us. Confucius said, "Choose a job you love, and you'll never work a day in your life."

Unfortunately, many of us spend our lives feeling trapped or bogged down by our work instead. For the majority of adults, most of the time in the day is spent working to earn our keep, feed our families, and take care of our other financial "necessities." We experience fun and fulfillment only when we escape.

But we can do better.

## Don't Let Work Bore You

In some cases, the solution is to simply find a better work situation, start your own business, or otherwise throw off the chains of your un-fun work and do something more productive with your life. In other cases, a different solution is required.

Whatever the situation, finding a fulfilling life's work and making it a financially viable option will rarely happen overnight.

It can take years of hard work and effort to make a life for yourself once you've found a working system to get you there.

But you still have to eat in the meantime, and this shouldn't mean you have to hate your life until you get to the end of the tunnel. Like eating three meals a day, fun is something we all need in regular and recurring doses.

Fortunately, there are steps you can take to make life much more bearable and even excellent as you journey toward your biggest dreams and truest fulfillment.

Healthy competition is one way to make a game out of your work, and games are a fantastic way to bring out the "play" in you and make work fun. Lorii Myers teaches, "In life, as in sports and any other game, healthy competition prevails—you come out to play and you play to win. You make it happen!"[1]

> Healthy competition is one way to make a game out of your work.

## Fun *Brings* Energy

As you create scenarios of good competition in your work place, you will find fun and games popping out all around you, and you'll start to come alive in ways you hadn't thought possible.

When appropriate (and *only* then), involve coworkers and colleagues in your games, and the whole office can experience new levels of excitement and engagement in their work.

Since transforming work into play makes work more fun for most involved, it also has another excellent result: it tends to make people work harder, faster, better, and more, often without even feeling like they're spending more energy on it.

This is because they are also *getting* energy from the endeavor. That's the power of fun. It *brings* energy!

When people are having fun, it doesn't seem like work, and when it doesn't seem like work, people are generally more willing and excited to dedicate their time and energy to it.

> When people are having fun, it doesn't seem like work, and when it doesn't seem like work, people are generally more willing and excited to dedicate their time and energy to it.

Just as many rush home after work to spend time doing what they enjoy, when people enjoy doing their work, they will be excited to rush *toward it!*

The key idea in all this is to turn your tedious or even undesirable tasks into fun and engaging games. When you're playing a fun game, you forget about the bad parts of your situation and really focus on the positive.

### *Enjoy* the Dreaded "Kids' Table"

Chris Brady shares the story of how one of his kids' friends changed something as mundane as sitting at the "kids' table" into a fun game that turned the whole situation around.

The families were vacationing together, and as often happens in large groups of families, the dinner situation was split up between "grown-ups" and "kids-only" tables.

Now if you've ever sat at the kids' table, you probably remember that you didn't feel you belonged there. All the other kids were noisy and annoying to adults, but your level of maturity was clearly far beyond your years. Yet there you were.

As Chris explains, one kid didn't sit around feeling sorry for himself and his demeaning position. Instead, he turned the evening meal into a game that all the kids could enjoy, thus rallying them, making them forget their woes, and creating a lot of fun for everyone there!

Here's what the kids-only dinner utensil game looked like: All the large cooking and baking utensils were taken out of the drawer and scattered on the counter. Then the kids drew straws to see which utensil was theirs. The utensil they drew became the only one they could use to eat their meal that night.

The leadership and insight of this young boy who took the initiative to turn life into a game produced an excellent icebreaker for those who were just getting to know one another. And the kids had loads of fun as they tried to eat their mac 'n' cheese with spatulas and tongs.

Some of the adults probably felt a little envious that they had to sit at the grown-ups' table.

## Want More, Work More

We challenge you to make eating with the little kids and tackling your "must-dos" and all the other work in your life a game or somehow fun in other ways. When you do, you and those you involve in your fun will spend lots of time thinking about how you can make your team stronger, what you can do to improve your performance, and what possible progress you can make in the overall efficiency and effectiveness of the whole undertaking.

People like to win games, and when that's how they view their work, they will lavish a lot more thought, energy, effort, and creativity on it—followed by action, implementation, and innovation. That's leadership. Fun and leadership are inexorably connected, as every kindergarten teacher knows—and as every top executive *should* know.

### Lead Well: Make the Game a Thing

If you're a leader, try to help consistently create a fun, competitive, game-like environment to inspire your people to love what they do and do it well. Dondi Scumaci said, "Play to win, not 'not to lose.'"

As Orrin Woodward and Oliver DeMille teach in their book *LeaderShift,* in an era of national decline, many people play a game of "How can I do the least amount of work and still not lose?"[2]

Getting ahead of this and making it much better to actually *win* is something leaders can do to drastically improve the energy and performance of the people they work with.

If you're not the leader in your workplace, and even if you don't yet care about the effectiveness of the team, you can probably at least see the good in your own increased enjoyment of work—having the hours pass more quickly instead of dragging on in boredom or frustration.

As is often true, whoever and wherever you are, you can make a huge difference in this by simply making the change in yourself. As Michael P. Naughton said, "Be the competition you wish to see in the world."

## Start a Competition

Even if you're not in a position to start creating company-wide competitions or incentives, you can start by competing with yourself. Just *see* how much better you can do this month than you did last.

Start secretly competing with the people around you, perhaps aiming toward being the best in your department, team, or field of work for this month. Make it a game. Give yourself rewards. Go for it!

Even if you can't officially start something, as people see you target big goals and hit them, they'll naturally want to start competing with you. And then the race is on!

Now that's fun!

Sometimes the most motivating experience is seeing someone who is supposedly your equal consistently hitting new levels of achievement and excellence. As you continually do exactly that, with a smile on your face, people will catch on to the game.

> Sometimes the most motivating experience is seeing someone who is supposedly your equal consistently hitting new levels of achievement and excellence.

So whether you're at the top of the company, at the bottom, or somewhere in between, try making work more fun by making it a competition—a game. This really works! As

James J. Freeland put it, "Pleasure and business, unlike water and oil, can sometimes be mixed."[3]

### Practicing Your Competitive Fun

Another important lesson about competition is that as you apply it to other aspects of life, such as your friendships, your fitness, and so on, you actually are able to produce another interesting effect in those areas.

For example, while hanging out with friends is one level of interesting fun and occasionally helps lift you toward your life goals, it usually only goes so far. But as you apply the principle of healthy competition to your friendships, you'll often find that both you and your friends begin accomplishing more goals—and having way more fun than when you were content with a TV show or a trip to the mall.

Whether your competition is over some deep and crucial task or project on which your future success and happiness hinges or simply a friendly rivalry that leads to hours of calculated thought, planning, and scheming, it can be really beneficial for your personal skills development, your friendship, and your overall fun in life.

# RANDOM FUN :)

*A bus station is where a bus stops. A*
*train station is where a train stops. On*
*my desk, I have a work station.*
~William Faulkner

For example, Chris Brady shared the following thoughts about how healthy competition and rivalry with his good friend and business partner Tim Marks have enriched his life and helped him practice skills such as innovation, ingenuity, and inspiration:

> *Tim is so prankishly funny. We've had this one partic-*
> *ular running gag, about white boots, that's been going on*
> *for years! It's so hilarious, and we both have so much fun*
> *with it!*
>
> *It started back in 2003 when Tim and I bought a couple*
> *of dirt bikes together. I have been riding and racing my*
> *whole life, while Tim is merely athletic and a quick study*
> *at anything he picks up. So in no time at all Tim was*
> *able to pretty much keep up with me and go everywhere*
> *I went.*
>
> *However, at some point Tim noticed that I was wearing*
> *a very expensive pair of motocross racing boots—built*

entirely out of white leather. White boots are worn by just about every top motocross racer and have long been in style.

Of course, these facts were lost on Tim, who picked up on it and began teasing me about wearing "girls' boots" to ride my motorcycle. We have gone back and forth on this for literally a decade, often in front of large crowds with slides and Photoshopped photos.

My favorite comeback is that Tim spent so much time on the ground (from crashing), that of course, he would be closer to my feet and have extra time to notice my boot color. Also, I have retorted that he seems to be as into footwear as any girl, even noticing what his motorcycle riding partner is wearing (a very girlish thing to notice).

Tim has countered with hilarious Photoshopped images, etc. Then, one time, I even went into a motorcycle shop and arranged ahead of time to shoot a video. In the video, I walk in and interview a "boot selling expert" about which type of boots are for which type of rider.

He played along great and showed the black boots were "definitely for slower riders, like, even just beginners." I showed this video at a major business conference. Tim is up on me lately, though, and I've got to get some good comeback for a future event. Great fun.

Tim and I also lived across the street from each other for about two years. One night I snuck into his garage and put a magazine cutout photo of a cheap pop-up camper affixed to the speedometer of his car, with the caption written underneath it, "Someday." Tim was dream building at *the time on expensive motor coaches and I called them "campers," much to his chagrin.*

*Tim, who teases me all the time for how much I love salt (and eat it out of the bottom of a bag of potato chips), fashioned a coat hanger to the handlebars of my motorcycle (in my garage late one night) with a bag of salt hanging from it as incentive for me to ride faster! One other time I came home to find an entire salt lick sitting in my garage.*

*Tim, for years, couldn't tie a necktie. So he had all of them pre-tied and hanging that way in his closet. I thought about (but never did it) going into his closet and untying them all, OR retying them so that they fell too short on his belly. I could just imagine Tim heading out the door, late for a meeting, with no way to adjust his tie!*

*Anyway, you can get a good feel for the fun we have by just these few stories, and there are hundreds more!*

## Use Your Fun to Feed Your Mind

It's interesting to note, and easy to see, that all this ridiculous fun was an excellent way for these two guys to bond and enjoy life. Some of those hearing these stories for the first time might wonder if Chris—or Tim, for that matter—is a comedian or a trickster.

Actually, they are both highly successful business leaders and executives. This makes their story even more poignant. Success and fun often go together—especially the kind of competitive fun that these leaders engage in.

Frankly, creating a running gag or a prank war (when it

> Success and fun often go together—especially the kind of competitive fun that leaders engage in.

stays appropriate, clean, and fun for everyone involved) is a truly fantastic way to improve your problem-solving skills, your creativity, your initiative and ingenuity, your ability to PDCA (Plan, Do, Check, Adjust), and many other vital aspects of leadership and success.

Not only do you get to employ them in an entertaining and exciting way on a regular basis, but you get to use them in a safe environment that's perfect for beginners and early learners. And, of course, it's also a ton of fun and a great exercise for the seasoned veterans in the whole process.

## Better Work and Better Play

By understanding and using these principles and techniques, you'll really be increasing both the fun and the effectiveness of your day-to-day efforts and experiences and, ultimately, the fun and the effectiveness of your life.

Making work fun naturally makes it flow better, helping

> Making work fun naturally makes it flow better, helping you accomplish more.

you accomplish more. And if you make the time you dedicate purely to fun a learning tool that leverages the great lessons hidden away in the nature of competition, then even in your play time, you'll be becoming a more effective leader and doer.

Competition really has this power. As you capitalize on it, you will have better work and better play—better fun that accomplishes better results.

In short, using competition to increase life's fun is like giving yourself an extra push in the right direction. There's stuff you've got to do in life, so make it count!

## BITE-SIZE FUN

Have a coupon contest. Call the family together and tell them that for the next week, everyone should find the best coupons they can. Then, a week from now, meet again and compare what you found. Whoever saves the family the most money, on something you actually need, gets a prize! Make the prize something everyone wants. Or alternatively, give a prize to everyone if all the coupons save the family a certain amount, such as $50 or more.

## CHAPTER THREE

# Friendship

*There is nothing better than a friend,*
*unless it is a friend with chocolate.*

~LINDA GRAYSON

Friendship is completely fun. Since we've already established that laughter and competition are fun, it's not really that big of a leap to suggest that laughing and competing with your best or closest friends would be pretty fun as well. The same is also true for the other fun pursuits in the world.

In fact, in many cases, the most fun *activities* are even more fun when they are done with the most fun *people*. And even if they aren't the most fun people, if they're your friends, the enjoyment of each activity

> The most fun *activities* are even more fun when they are done with the most fun *people*.

or experience can be amplified by their presence and participation.

Just as the friendships themselves are made more enjoyable by applying these excellent principles of fun, the results are better when applied by a group of close-knit friends.

Basically, if you're going to do fun things—or even difficult things—they'll probably be more fun with your friends than without them, and your interactions with these friends will be a whole lot more enjoyable if you make a point of having fun together.

This is not a shocking revelation to most people, yet too often, we forget to do fun things with fun people and to make hard tasks more enjoyable by doing them with our friends.

For most of us, just being with a friend makes life more fun. That's why we call a specific person our friend, rather than some random guy with a goofy haircut.

Since we so easily have increased levels of fun with these people, imagine what kind of super-fun we could experience if we combined their already attractive and enjoyable nature with the kind of activities, projects, and attitudes that naturally increase fun on their own.

This is the kind of friendship that men like Aristotle and C. S. Lewis wrote about and sought throughout their lives, and it's also the kind we recommend to people who want to really have fun in life as well as accomplish an important mission and role in society.

## The Most Rewarding Hobby

Chris Brady called pursuing and cultivating great friendships the most rewarding hobby. This is what he said:

*People are endlessly interesting. Everyone has a story, a history, a network, a past, and a future. Each one of us was a cute little baby once, and we've all also had our uglier moments.*

*May I suggest a way to entertain yourself endlessly? Learn to initiate new friendships, cultivate old ones, and in short, make a sport of investing your life into the lives of others.*

*Sound a little too "touchy-feely"? Maybe. But I give you my personal guarantee that it will be one of the most rewarding, fulfilling, stimulating, interesting, entertaining, and worthwhile things you've ever done.*

> "Learn to initiate new friendships, cultivate old ones, and in short, make a sport of investing your life into the lives of others."
> ~Chris Brady

*It will become your new sport, hobby, pastime, and focus. The more you get interested in others, the more you'll discover about this world in which we live and the better you will understand yourself.*

*You're already into this, you say? Fine. Can you step it up a bit? Can you seek to add more value to everyone you meet? Can you grow in your "other-focussedness"? (How's that for a word?)*

> "You'll never regret the times when you sincerely take an interest in other people."
> ~Chris Brady

*Do so, and you'll never regret it. In fact, I would go so far as to say that you'll never regret the times when you sincerely take an interest in other people.*

*It may not always be returned in kind, it might not appear to bear any fruit whatsoever, but the giving of your attention, affirmation, and appreciation to another human being always boomerangs back around to you.*

*Try it and see. I dare you.*

## True Friendship Is Love in Motion

Brady continued:

*There are thousands of books on money, business, marriage, child rearing, diet, exercise, cooking, and gardening. Strange, however, is the relative scarcity of those on the subject of friendship.*

*A little over a year ago, my bride underwent brain surgery to remove a large tumor. It was physically traumatic, life-threatening, and very scary. Terri emerged from the experience healthy and armed with yet another obvious blessing straight from God.*

*Ordeals such as that demonstrate a lot of things. First, they have a staggering power to realign one's priorities. And secondly, they reveal the real friends in one's life.*

*There were callers and well-wishers, people sending meals, others sending cards. Several showed up in the waiting room and rode shotgun through the entire day of surgery, some returning the next morning, others staying the night.*

*Terri had a nurse friend assist in the recovery room the first night, and another awaiting her arrival at our house upon her hospital discharge.*

*From the moment she arrived home until several weeks after, Terri received around-the-clock care from an army of girlfriends who had mobilized, scheduled themselves, and swooped onto the scene to nurture, support, administer medication, provide child care, and just "be there."*

*It was awesome.*

*It was love in motion.*

*It was true friendship.*

*Friendship is hard to define. It has no official commitments like marriage. It has no familial ties like parenthood or relationships with siblings. It carries no consistent definitions.*

*But like great art, while defying description, it is readily identifiable when it is experienced.*

*Terri's surgery was a reminder to us both of the value of true friendships in our life. We treasure the incredible people God has placed around us, and we pray that we are as good a friend to them as they have been to us.*

*Friendships should never be taken for granted, as they provide grounding, comfort, companionship, depth, meaning, and enjoyment. Now's*

> "Like great art, while defying description, [true friendship] is readily identifiable when it is experienced."
> ~Chris Brady

*a great time to give some consideration to the friendships in your life. Nurture them.*

*Invest. Contribute. Serve. Laugh, live, and forge tighter the relationships that truly are one of life's greatest treasures.*

### But What about the Fun Factor?

It is important to understand the rewarding nature of the friendship-building hobby and also the depth and comfort that friendship can bring to your life in times of trial or difficulty. In many ways, these are both just deeper shades of fun.

As you seek friends who are also on the path to greatness and success, you'll have much to connect about that's meaningful, deep, and ultimately rewarding. But it goes further than that.

Not only will you be able to have the level of depth that means real and lasting connection on things that matter, but with the *best* friendships, you'll also find the best simple fun and enjoyment that life has to offer.

> Not only will you able to have the level of depth that means real and lasting connection on things that matter, but with the *best* friendships, you'll also find the best simple fun and enjoyment that life has to offer.

Friendship is about more than the deep connections of cause and character—though these can't be ignored; it's also about the *fun* you have together.

Think back to the stories shared in the last chapter and the chapter on laughter regarding the fun Chris Brady has with Tim Marks and the fun Orrin Woodward has with his friends and business partners.

Having good friendships can lead to years and years of good fun, and when you make a point of developing stronger, deeper, and better friendships, you'll find that life itself is more fun.

Sometimes your fun shared activities will be service projects in your community, while other times, they'll be competitions to achieve some big new goal for work. Sometimes your fun will be just that: fun. You'll play together, tease each other, and simply enjoy each other's company.

As your relationships include a wide variety of meaningful and engaging activities, you'll be learning and growing together in ways that are incredibly fun.

So go do something new with your friends! Reconnect with an old friend you haven't talked to in a while. Make a new friend. Play a harmless prank on a close friend and laugh together about it. Make a fool of yourself with friends. Plan a surprise for a friend.

Do something today to celebrate and cultivate the wonderful friendships in your life.

# BITE-SIZE FUN

Start a friendly debate with someone close to you about one of the great questions of modern life. Not the one about the tree falling in the forest. The other one: What should a person eat first on a chocolate bunny—the tail or the ears? Make the debate last.

:)

CHAPTER FOUR

# Fitness

*A bear, however hard he tries,*
*grows tubby without exercise.*

~A. A. MILNE

You may have wondered about the prologue to this book, where top leader, effective businessman, and successful husband and father Orrin Woodward shared the story of a group of business colleagues playing a series of basketball games.

As intense as that was, there is more to the story, and it brilliantly illustrates the power of using competition and laughter to change gym time from hard and annoying work that simply "has to be done" to one of the most enjoyable and rewarding aspects of life:

*This summer, because I desired to stay in shape but loathe treadmills or any other fitness activity not involving competition, I asked my friend Bill Lewis if he thought some of his top business partners would be interested in a little three-on-three driveway basketball.*

*At the time, I had no idea what a big part of the summertime fun this would become. It was amazing. Bill Lewis, Holger Spiewak, Aron Radosa, Kirk Birtles, Steve Morgan, and I became engrossed in a basketball war in a best-of-seven series that will be talked about for years.*

*It all started when we divided the teams into what we called the PC Members (the old guys) and the Band of Brothers (the younger guys). This created two teams that refused to back down, let down, or stay down.*

*In fact, within minutes of the start of the first game, I realized that shooting around with my teenagers was not proper preparation for the level of intensity required to compete in these games. Not surprisingly, my timing was off the whole first day as I attempted to adjust to the level of competition.*

## Fun Exercise!

*My teammates, on the other hand, picked up the slack. Holger Spiewak, despite not knowing the game of basketball, had starred as a soccer player in his younger days, and his athleticism reminded me of a young Dennis Rodman with the Detroit Pistons. However, the quintessential basketball player and stalwart of the PC team was Bill Lewis.*

*His playing on opening day carried us to victory as his outside jump-shot, inside drives, and quick passes allowed the PC team to win all three games. After the games, I suggested maybe we could do it again on Thursday, and an epic series was born.*

I believed, since we won each of the first three games, we would really hurt them on Thursday after I started playing at the new rhythm and speed of the game. My thinking, however, foolishly missed one very important point, namely, the PDCA (Plan, Do, Check, Adjust) process.

The Band of Brothers (BoB) consisted of three great athletes who understand and implement the PDCA process daily into their work and family lives. With the inside/outside combination of Radosa and Birtles, a competitive series was guaranteed as these two relentless rebounders packed solid muscle on their chiseled nearly 200-pound frames.

The final BoB opponent was Steve Morgan. This gentleman did play basketball in high school (and in pickup games across Michigan) and thus quarterbacked his team. His knowledge of the game allowed him to make the needed adjustments to check our strategies. This ensured that neither team would run away with this series and that every victory would be earned.

Steve played the point guard position, distributing the ball to whoever had the hot hand. And if we relaxed at all on defense, he would drive right past us for easy hoops. Above all, Steve's killer instinct, upping his intensity and focus when the game was on the line, made each game into a war. Nonetheless, because of our impressive victory during day one, I was lulled into passivity and only awoke after the BoB storm of day two.

## Victory, Defeat, and Drama

*Day after day, we played. If one team won the day, the other team would regroup, make plans, and win the next time we played. This went on and on.*

*One great thing about winners is they never get comfortable with losing. In fact, show me anyone who is comfortable losing, and I will show you someone who loses consistently.*

*As a side note, during all this, I sort of lost track of things—in a good way. I was so focused on those games, they were so fun, that my whole life just improved!*

*I took my cheery attitude to work, to family time, and to every aspect of my life. I just naturally applied the energy of this overwhelming fun to everything.*

*The final game started with baskets trading back and forth, and it was tied at four points apiece at the first water break. The BoB, however, surged out of the break, scoring three unanswered baskets to take a commanding 7–4 lead.*

*The next set of events I experienced in slow motion, although the game pace was extremely fast on the court. Holger passed the ball to me, and I quickly launched a bomb from downtown that hit the mark, making it 7–5.*

*It was time to execute a series of flawless pick-and-rolls and end this game, or we would have to confront the BoB again on day seven. We played on and on, with major intensity.*

## Carpe Diem!

I quickly dribbled to the top of the key, hoping to catch the BoB napping, to take a quick shot. I turned to face the hoop and made eye contact with Steve Morgan, in a dead sprint toward me. I made up my mind to shoot anyway and arced a moon ball that took forever to come down. Somehow the shot just avoided the outstretched hands of Morgan, and he turned around just in time to see the ball swish through the net. The PC team was up 10–8 with just one more point to go!

Bill released the potential game-winning shot that just missed, but Holger's offensive rebounding gave us two more shots at victory. Incredibly, both layups rolled on the rim but refused to fall. Three game-winning shots, in other words, but no points!

The BoB rebounded and took possession. Steve, guarded by me, dribbled to the right to lead me into Kirk's screen. However, as Kirk attempted to roll, one of his calf muscles popped, and he collapsed in pain on the court.

He was not getting back up, and just like that, the series and the summer were over due to an injury. Since we were leading by the required two points, the game ended in our victory, by an injury forfeit, winning day six by two games to one and the series four days to two. Thankfully, Kirk, who is a former physical therapist, recovered nicely.

This was incredibly fun! It made the whole summer exciting.

*I thoroughly enjoyed myself in this series. Looking back, I think the key lesson each of the players took away from it was how much fun it can be to incorporate the PDCA process into life. When winners get together to compete, it promises to be a great time.*

*In all the games, no one trash-talked, gave cheap shots, or cheated. Instead, it was just competition at the highest of levels among friends and business partners.*

## Can't Wait to Exercise?

As we learn from this experience, by applying the other principles of fun to undertakings in life that seem less than exciting in their normal form, we can reframe and transform tasks we dislike into pastimes that we love. Remember, this entire story began with a man who just wanted to make his daily exercise more fun.

When we labor for fun, not only will we be excited about doing activities we weren't thrilled about before, but we'll turn them into some of the most fun and rewarding pursuits around.

In this story, Woodward shows that they not only met their physical fitness goals and needs, but they actually managed to maximize their personal growth and character building by applying the powerful principles they had learned in other parts of their lives. They applied principles of business leadership to physical exercise and principles of fitness to better business success.

Here are some ways to do the same in your life:

- Invite a friend to play racquetball every Thursday before work.
- Go jogging with your dog.
- Ride your exercise bike until halftime while watching a football game.
- Play backyard soccer with the neighborhood kids on Friday evening.
- Join an intramural volleyball team.
- Challenge a friend to run a half-marathon with you and begin training together.

Oh, and you can also get special white leather boots for motorcycle racing, which are far superior to other kinds of riding boots. Or you can tie potato-chip bags full of salt between your handlebars in order to make yourself drive faster, seeking more salt in your diet. Just sayin'…

As you make fitness part of your planned fun, you'll hit two birds with one stone—checking off the exercise box on your list and spending some truly valuable time in pure enjoyment with family, friends, or colleagues. You'll be creating deep and lasting bonds while making powerful and impactful health and fitness choices.

Make fitness fun. Applying the principles of fun to exercise makes your whole life brighter, easier, and better!

# BITE-SIZE FUN

Go to a park and swing on a swing. Take your spouse, or go alone. Swing for a long time, and remember why you used to love doing this when you were a kid.

## CHAPTER FIVE

# Seasons

*I know it is wet, and the sun is not sunny,*
*but we can have lots of good fun that is funny.*

~DR. SEUSS

O ne of the most common fun killers in our modern world, and frankly one of the easiest ones to banish from our lives, is the tendency to buzz through life without *noticing* the fun all around us.

Especially in the world of business and success chasing, it's easy to get caught up in what makes us busy without taking time to enjoy what makes it all worth the effort. And when you ignore the things that make your hard work worth doing, you're generally left feeling that it *isn't* worth doing.

> When you ignore the things that make your hard work worth doing, you're generally left feeling that it *isn't* worth doing.

This type of unfulfillment is just not fun. Yet the solution is curiously simple.

## Stop and Smell the Roses

This old American cliché can be the key to opening a whole new can of fun in your life, and truly understanding and applying its meaning will literally revolutionize the way you interact with fun.

The story goes that one woman spent all her time culti-vating and nurturing a beautiful rose garden; it was her life's work. She spent hours and hours each day trimming here, watering there, and making everything in her garden perfect.

Yet in doing this, she spent so much time *working* in her garden that she never actually took a moment to *enjoy* the fruits of her labors. Her diligence and attention to detail were certainly commendable, yet there was clearly some-thing missing in her approach.

One day, her dear friend came to visit the garden and was delighted by the beauty of the flowers and the loveli-ness of their fragrance. The garden was truly spectacular. It was a place of real beauty, capable of inspiring life and joy in the beholder in ways that aren't often found in the modern world.

As this friend basked in the delights of the garden, she noticed her friend the gardener, as always, working away at some task or another. She had accomplished such a glorious work, yet her face was unhappy and unsatisfied as she tweaked a branch here or a petal there.

The friend frowned a bit and looked around. Yes, there was something missing here, but it was not in the flowers or the walks, which were all purely delicious to anyone who came to them. It was in the face of the gardener, in the way she held her head, and in the way she slumped her shoulders. She was being broken by her work, even though she had every reason to rejoice in it.

> She was being broken by her work, even though she had every reason to rejoice in it.

Gently, the friend approached the gardener and took the watering can she had just picked up. Setting it on a nearby bench, she put her arm around the gardener's drooping shoulders and guided her to the center of the garden—a beautiful gazebo with the prettiest vines and roses in the entire garden all around the immaculate white benches.

They sat there, and the friend looked into the weary eyes of the gardener and softly spoke, "My dear friend, when was the last time you stopped and smelled the roses?"

## Don't Miss the Point

When you forget to stop and smell the roses in your beautiful garden, you forget to have fun on the journey. Often our work is paying off right in front of our eyes, but if we never open them, we miss a lot of paydays.

Smelling the roses is the fun part of creating a beautiful rose garden. Walking through the paths, sitting on the benches, listening to the birds, and drinking in the essence of the garden are what makes the weeding, watering, pruning, and taming of the place a blessing instead of a chore.

If you want life to be fun, you really have to stop ignoring the fun parts. Of course we're not saying you should just sit around waiting for perfect roses to magically spring up around you for your pleasure and enjoyment. We're also not saying that once you've made a nice garden, you should spend all your time watching it die off and fall into disrepair and wilderness.

Yet if you never drink in the smell of roses, your roses aren't worth nearly as much as they could be. In fact, the whole point of having a glorious garden is being able to really enjoy it.

It comes down to this: well-kept gardens are not complete if they're never enjoyed by the gardener who looks around and says, "Well done."

> The whole point of having a glorious garden is being able to really enjoy it.

An unenjoyed garden is, and always will be, an incomplete one. The same is true of a life. More to the point, such an unenjoyed life will be an extremely un-*fun* one.

So smell those roses! Keep watering and weeding and perfecting, but have fun doing it! There are plenty of things for you to enjoy, so don't let them escape your attention.

> Don't focus so hard on being perfect that you forget to be fun.

Don't focus so hard on being perfect that you forget to be fun.

True perfection actually *includes* perfect fun, so as long as you leave fun out of the picture, you'll never really reach perfection. Just smell the roses already!

# RANDOM FUN :)

*With sufficient thrust,*
*pigs fly just fine.*
~Source Unknown

### *Find* the Fragrance

In his book *Hardwiring Happiness*,[1] Rick Hanson, Ph.D., explains an excellent way to keep ourselves consistently smelling the roses in meaningful ways. He teaches the importance of *creating* positive experiences and memories by dwelling on them as they happen.

As he puts it, "If you take care of the minutes, the years will take care of themselves." So how do you take care of the minutes?

Hanson teaches one particular technique that we think is absolutely brilliant! It's a great way to instantly and easily increase the fun in your life, by capturing it as it happens. Here's how he explains it:

*While I was in college I stumbled across something that seemed remarkable then, and still seems remarkable to me now. Some small thing would be happening. It could be a few guys saying, "Come on, let's go get some pizza," or a young woman smiling at me. Not a big deal. But I found that if I let the good fact become a good experience, not just an idea, and then stayed with it for at least a few breaths, not brushing it off or moving on fast to something else, it felt like something good was sinking into me, becoming a part of me. In effect, I was taking in the good—a dozen seconds at a time. It was quick, easy, and enjoyable. And I started feeling better.*

Imagine how doing this with little things in your life could increase your fun and happiness.

Hanson goes on to explain that sometimes fun is as simple as eating an orange, but only if you do it right. He quotes the following example in his book:

*I love to take in the good whenever I eat an orange. I have at least two a day, so I get an opportunity to experience this moment often. As I break through the skin, I gently close my eyes and breathe in the sweet scent. I hold that pleasure in my mind and think about how I am the first person ever to see inside this orange and taste its fruit. Although this experience takes less than a minute, it has an enormously positive effect on my mood and energy level. I look forward to it throughout the day.*

The small example of this man actually has a number of different lessons in it, all of which can really help us smell the roses and make the little things in life tons of fun.

The first important lesson we want to notice is that he specifically says he has this chance every day—more than once. Often, we take the little actions we do several times a day and turn them into boring routine, when we could be using them to create frequent opportunities for real fun!

This is really powerful because what makes a routine event boring in our experience turns it into *better* fun in his. He looks at the frequency of this action not as something that makes it common or monotonous, but as a blessing that makes it abundant and bountiful!

So instead of saying he doesn't enjoy it anymore because it's too "normal," he instead triumphs in this assurance that he'll get to take pleasure in *something* quite often, since he knows how to enjoy oranges and he eats them frequently. This truly *is* remarkable!

What are some of the activities you do regularly in your daily routine? Is there some way you could apply this technique to those tiny little things to make your life more fun?

How could you make driving to and from work an exciting event in your life? Here are some suggestions for making the routine in your life more fun:

- Pay with all coins at a place where they are mostly used to credit cards.
- Listen to songs on random shuffle on your iPod.
- Take a different route to work.

- Switch cars with your spouse for a week.
- Change where everyone sits around the dinner table or when riding in the car together.
- Have an "upside-down" meal, beginning with dessert first.
- Initiate a homemade gift exchange for Christmas with your extended family.
- Take a break at work by watching funny YouTube videos with your staff.
- Think of a harmless prank to play on a friend.
- Host a scavenger hunt with your friends on New Year's Eve.
- Go golfing with only three clubs.
- Have a Lego building contest with your kids.
- Teach your grandmother a rap song.
- Buy five magazines at random and flip through them.

Try this kind of exercise out on your various little activities and just *see* if it doesn't make life more fun. We're betting it will.

Another important lesson in this story is the value of having fun with the simple things in life. The fact is we generally see a lot more of the simple things than we do the elaborate or highly extravagant ones. That said, learning to enjoy the simple things is a good way to ensure that you'll keep having fun in life.

> Learning to enjoy the simple things is a good way to ensure that you'll keep having fun in life.

Learn to enjoy an orange—to revel in the fact that you're the first and possibly the only one to see inside or taste it. When you can make *that* fun, your life is going to be absolutely *drenched* in fun orange juice.

The "Bite-Size Fun" portions of this book are a great place to find additional guidelines and techniques for making simple things fun. So use them! We promise it'll be worth it to master this principle in your life!

## So...What about "Seasons"?

You might be starting to wonder why this chapter is called "Seasons," since we really haven't mentioned them at all. Well, let's get to it then.

Another important aspect of smelling the roses, aside from learning to enjoy the little things in your day-to-day life by paying attention to them and appreciating the simple, is learning to take notice of the important opportunities for fun around you that are only available for a limited time.

If you want to really make the most of your fun in life, you should make a point of paying attention to what seasonal fun can be had today that might be missed by putting it off for too long. For example, taking a drive with your family to see the colorful autumn leaves is rather difficult to do in the dead of winter or at the onset of spring.

Likewise, opportunities for a snowball fight with your kids don't often present themselves in late summer, and a hike ending with a dip in the lake is better in warm weather than in freezing temperatures. Or maybe you like polar bear swimming. If so, winter is the best time for it.

When the weather *does* permit, these seasonal activities are often some of the most fun pastimes around. As we mentioned earlier, a picnic is generally more fun than eating at a restaurant. A hike is usually more entertaining than watching television.

Playing basketball or catch with your teen is almost always more fun than going out for a burger. Or, if not, go out for a burger.

Reading to your kids by the fire is often more enjoyable than a movie. And having a snowball fight or taking a drive to see the changing leaves is definitely more exciting than just sitting around trying to think of something fun to do.

## Life Seasons

Likewise, there are seasons of our life as well as seasons of the year. Different activities are fun during these various life seasons. For example, what you like to do most as a kid typically changes when you become a teen.

The same is generally true when single adults get married. These life seasons bring lots of new opportunities for fun as we mature. The older we get, the more designed gratification we may need!

Think about your current season of life, and make a list of anything that you'll miss when you get older. Then do more of this while it's still great fun.

Get your friends and kids involved in this same process, and the merriment will really increase. No season should be without fun.

In short, create a new personal habit that becomes a key part of your life: Keep your eyes open. And start smelling the seasonal roses!

> Enjoy the little things, each one in its season, and don't ignore the fun that's right in front of you.

Enjoy the little things, each one in its season, and don't ignore the fun that's right in front of you. Don't be the killjoy who wouldn't know fun if it handed him a mitt and tossed him the ball. Live a little. Trust us; it's more fun that way.

# BITE-SIZE FUN

"I am at my computer with a mug of coffee when my husband leaves for work. He kisses the top of my head and I say a quick 'bye' over my shoulder as I scan the headlines, the weather forecast, the e-mails that have multiplied overnight like mold spores. It's not until I look out the window and see him climbing into the car that I realize what's missing. And what's missing is me—my attention, my presence, my here-and-now connection with the love of my life. 'Wait,' I yell, and he looks up and smiles. I run out in my bath-robe, throw my arms around him, kiss his mouth and cheek. 'Good-bye!' I say, and he laughs and kisses me back. 'Good-bye.'"*

Now try it yourself!

*"Life Is Good…Don't Miss It!" by Catherine Newman, March 2010 Ladies' Home Journal

## What Is Leisure?

Benjamin Franklin was famous for various sayings contrasting leisure and laziness, making it clear that they are two very separate and *different* things.

That said, real leisure must encompass more than mere "lack of occupation" or even "idleness," both of which are terms used in many modern dictionaries to define leisure.

> Real leisure must encompass more than mere "lack of occupation" or even "idleness."

Leisure means that you are *actively involved*, while mere entertainment *happens* to you. Leisure is active; entertainment is passive. Entertainment is done to or for you.

In addition, leisure is different from laziness or entertainment in at least three important ways.

The first is that in leisure, you actually *create* value, along with partaking of value, because you're engaging in an active behavior that's inherently productive. Entertainment, in contrast, consists of merely consuming value created by others and consistently expecting them to provide you with more and more of it, while you sit on your couch doing nothing.

The second is that, even if what you are doing isn't directly connected to your life purpose or mission, real leisure activities always make you more prepared and better able to fulfill that purpose or mission. This happens for myriad reasons, depending on the specific activity, but whatever the method or reason, appropriate and real

# CHAPTER SIX

# Leisure

*If man is to be liberated to enjoy more leisure,*
*he must also be prepared to*
*enjoy this leisure fully and creatively.*

~Eleanor Roosevelt

One of the long-lost principles in our modern society is the idea of leisure. While many understand the idea of "taking a break" from work, they misunderstand the subtleties that separate passive entertainment from active recreation.

While it is true that leaving leisure out of your daily routine tends to lead to early burnout, it is equally true that a fundamental misunderstanding of what leisure really is tends to lead to a lot of wasted time, frivolity, and even personal decay.

In many ways, this concept is at the center of the whole fun problem—and also happens to be the primary solution.

leisure equips you to face the challenges, struggles, and tasks of successfully living a full and excellent life.

On the flip side, entertainment is something that actually distracts or even detracts from your larger goals, often leading you to be more and more caught up in entertainment and less and less likely to achieve your real purpose.

And third, leisure is actually fulfilling and naturally leads to a return to hard work and occupation, while entertainment never really satisfies and therefore leads to a greater, *longer* search for satisfaction in the fun department. And since dissatisfaction with entertainment rarely opens our eyes to the reality of actual leisure, this search generally turns into an endless downward spiral of dissatisfied and unproductive entertainment addiction or even overdose.

### "Whatcha Wanna Do?"

It's like the 1980 Johnny Lee song, "Lookin' for Love," which bemoans a man's wasted and unfulfilling life of "lookin' for love in all the wrong places."[1] In today's world, we have an unfortunate cultural inclination to be lookin' for fun in all the wrong places.

> In today's world, we have an unfortunate cultural inclination to be lookin' for fun in all the wrong places.

As long as we're searching for fun in mindless entertainment and all-out laziness, we're going to find something seriously lacking. And when "digging deeper" means simply getting deeper and deeper in the entertainment trap, we'll find ourselves always chasing fun but never really having much of it.

This is extremely unhelpful in nearly every way. In fact, with this philosophy, we end up like the buzzards from Disney's *The Jungle Book*: constantly asking each other what we're going to do yet seldom doing anything.

Sadly, this often means we do neither fun activities nor anything else. That is the danger of the entertainment trap. Since you never fill your fun box enough to make you feel ready to dive back into real and meaningful work, you actually end up losing both effective fun time and effective work time.

Yet understanding and living the principle of effective leisure is exactly the cure we've been looking for.

## Pick Leisure over Laziness

An easy first step is to start listing leisure activities and contrasting them with their entertainment counterparts.

> Playing sports is more of a leisure activity (and is therefore nearly always more fulfilling) than merely watching them.

For example, playing sports is more of a leisure activity (and is therefore nearly always more fulfilling) than merely watching them. Not that you should never even consider watching a ball game, but playing one with friends (as we saw in the prologue and in chapter 4) or with your kids is generally more fulfilling and naturally leads you back to your life's work, teaching you important principles and lessons along the way and also giving you opportunities for character development and real growth.

These results are less likely when you simply watch the game, which often tends to make you want to watch *more*, rather than sending you back where you need to be.

Similarly, reading a book frequently gives you real insight and preparation for your mission, helps you feel fulfilled, and naturally sends you back into battle when you're done, while watching television generally sucks you in and keeps you—even as the quality of what you're viewing declines.

Playing a good game of pretend with your younger children will usually give you more satisfaction and challenge your creative thinking and other leadership skills in more powerful ways than playing a video game.

> Playing a good game of pretend with your younger children will usually give you more satisfaction and challenge your creative thinking and other leadership skills in more powerful ways than playing a video game.

And again, it has a natural ending and makes you more motivated to work on the other things you care deeply about, while the video game usually just shuts the rest out and captures your complete focus—even when you know you have more important duties.

And the list goes on.

## Strengthening Key Relationships by Increasing Real Fun

It's also important to note that leisure activities often help you strengthen your key relationships, while giving in to entertainment frequently hurts them. This is significant.

Truly effective leaders—and in fact all who are truly successful—understand the importance of relationships and take steps to make them the priority they should be.

By sacrificing the self-centered and generally passive

> Truly effective leaders understand the importance of relationships and take steps to make them the priority they should be.

entertainments available for more excellent and *worthwhile* leisure activities, not only will you find yourself having much more fun, but it will naturally tend to be the kind that leads to meaningful and powerful relationships in all areas of life.

## Bit by Bit

Once you understand why this difference matters so much, and you've made yourself a list or set of guidelines to separate leisure from laziness, the next step is to start *choosing* leisure consistently in your day-to-day life.

As you come to really see the difference, you'll find that your life is significantly more fun—much *better*—when you spend it doing the right activities.

This isn't to say you'll be perfect from now on just because you know to pay attention. But when you *do* pay attention, you'll be faced with all sorts of opportunities to choose real leisure and fulfillment over the entertainment trap. At that point, it's a matter of making the right choices. As you do so, bit by bit, your life will get more and more fun!

Interestingly, leisure is like financial savings or investment, while entertainment is a lot like spending or using debt. Leisure brings energy and benefit to your life.

## The Four Choices of Leisure

Now in all this, it can be easy to get mad at what you're reading because you know you don't want to make the commitment, right here and now, to never watch a movie or a football game again.

Luckily, that's not what we're suggesting.

Achieving true leisure—which is an important part of life—doesn't have to mean giving up these types of activities altogether. It means consistently making four important choices to keep your fun real and productive:

### 1. *Choose Variety.*

To keep things *really* fun, you need to have a variety of different activities that you're actually doing. Just having a list of 100 incredibly fun leisure pastimes isn't enough. You have to actually *do* a bunch of them—on a regular basis.

Likewise, being perfectly consistent about doing the same two leisure activities every day is not the most effective way to have fun; in fact, it can often get boring.

So have a bunch of things on your list, and do them all! In the process, you'll find which are especially fun to you and which you don't need to repeat as often. You'll also be having tons of fun and learning all sorts of cool skills and lessons as you go!

# RANDOM FUN :)

*I never did a day's work in my life. It was all fun.*
~Thomas Edison

## 2. *Choose Balance.*

As you select activities, it's important to keep the proper balance in your variety.

We've said a few times that a picnic is more fun than a restaurant. While this is true, it doesn't mean you should never go to a restaurant or that doing so is always choosing entertainment over leisure.

Likewise, you should play many ball games with friends or family for every one you watch on TV, and you should read many hours for every movie you watch. Instead of just mindlessly listening to whatever is on the radio, listen to audios that really teach, inspire, and make you better. (This kind of listening is a very active brain activity.) Again, listen to at least nine hours of such powerful audios for every hour of simply surfing radio stations.

Of course this ratio isn't exact or strict, but it is an excellent guideline to keep you on track for real fun and productivity in life and leisure.

### 3.  *Choose Quality.*

Also, if you want to have the best possible fun, instead of choosing self-indulgent or lazy alternatives, you really have to make a priority of choosing high-quality activities. So when you *are* going to watch a movie, pick a 10.

Business leaders Mark and Jenn Paul teach this principle in relation to health and fitness: when you *are* going to break your diet or eat something unhealthy, a good way to keep yourself in check is to never settle for less than a 10 in terms of quality and how delicious your treat is.

> If you're going to feed your body something unhealthy, choose a delectable piece of German chocolate cake over a cup of M&Ms.

In other words, if you're going to feed your body something unhealthy, choose a delectable piece of German chocolate cake over a cup of M&Ms.

In fact, you should also apply this to the healthy things you're putting in as well.

In activities, whether it's a movie, a picnic, or a full-on vacation, always choose high-quality options, and there's always at least one available. For example, bestselling author Chris Brady's book *A Month of Italy: Rediscovering the Art of Vacation*[2] shows how travel is an enormously valuable leisure activity—and loads of fun. In fact, such activities create memories that are fun for the rest of your life.

Sometimes this goes back to balance: If you don't have a movie to watch that's a 10, it isn't time to watch a movie. Find a different activity that *is* a 10.

Making quality a priority in your life is one of the most important aspects of leisure, and it really will make a world of difference in the amount of real fun you have and the amount of benefit it actually gives you.

> Making quality a priority in your life is one of the most important aspects of leisure.

And obviously, until you truly commit to this, the quality of your fun and your life is going to suffer.

### 4.   *Choose to Activate the Activity.*

This applies especially to the few times you *do* choose to watch a movie or eat at a restaurant or do any other activity that's more naturally a consumer activity and less productive.

But you should also use it in the most obviously productive and active pursuits you can think of. In either case, doing so will increase the amount of fun you'll have and the amount of growth that will naturally come from each activity.

Activating the activity is taking a normally passive and consumer-oriented activity and turning it into an active one. For example, as we've already mentioned, when you want to go out on a date, choose a picnic rather than a restaurant. Or instead of just shopping, turn it into a daddy–daughter date with your twelve-year-old, and work to make it really fun for her.

A great way to accomplish this is to focus on building relationships. Again, this has to be done in the right variety, balance, and quality, but as you use different activities specifically to build key relationships, you'll be acting productively and in fun ways.

> If you are truly strengthening your vital relationships with an activity, it definitely falls under the definition of leisure.

An example of this might be the occasion when you *do* take your spouse to a nice restaurant and use your time there to engage in relationship-building conversation and bonding time.

If you are truly strengthening your vital relationships with an activity, it definitely falls under the definition of leisure.

## At Your Leisure!

As you come to more fully internalize these lessons and consistently make these four choices, your fun and the power of your leisure time will be increased in incredible and amazing ways.

This is not to say that there's never a time for real and deep relaxation. In fact, one of the main points of this book is to teach the importance of having fun and relaxation a lot more than we typically do. But we too often let our search for fun, relaxation, and renewal lead to escapism or self-indulgence. This isn't as much fun.

> We too often let our search for fun, relaxation, and renewal lead to escapism or self-indulgence. This isn't as much fun.

Understanding and applying the principles of leisure is a powerful cure. As more and more people come to find the true rejuvenation and fulfillment that can only come from *real* leisure, they will enjoy more fun! This will have a huge positive influence on every part of their lives.

# BITE-SIZE FUN

Give yourself a new rule: If there isn't something truly great on TV, you won't watch anything. If you follow this rule, your fun will soar!

:)

## CHAPTER SEVEN

# Reading

*What's cheaper than a gallon of gas? An ebook.*
*Save a dollar, stay home and read!*

~Shandy L. Kurth

The above quote is especially true because most of the great classics of humanity can be found as ebooks for very little cost. Many are even free!

If you want to add a bunch of fun to your life, to more fully and productively apply the principle of real leisure, and to increase your overall leadership success (or even if you want just *one* of these things), we have a suggestion for you: make a habit of consistent and voracious reading as well as listening to great audios.

Reading and listening are two of the most powerful ways to make the principle of real and

> Reading and listening are two of the most powerful ways to make the principle of real and present fun work toward building you a highly successful future.

present fun work toward building you a highly successful future.

If we told you there was something you could do that would add bucket loads of fun to your daily life and increase your ability to achieve your goals and ambitions at the same time, we know you'd be interested. That's why you're reading this book.

Well, like many of the other things discussed here, reading has just such an effect on those who make it a priority and approach it correctly.

The book *Turn the Page: How to Read Like a Top Leader*[1] from the LIFE Leadership Essentials Series is a great resource for learning to make your reading more fun and more effective at helping you get where you're trying to go. It's a hard-hitting combination of principles and techniques designed to make reading more enjoyable and you more likely to achieve targeted goals.

We highly recommend it to anyone seeking to learn to love and master the art of reading like a top leader—and who wants all the benefits that come from doing so.

With that said, let's talk about some of the reasons reading and listening are not only deeply important but also fun.

## Readers Are Leaders

One common attribute you'll find among history's most effective and beloved leaders is a strong background of solid reading. Most people who've had a truly remarkable impact on the world or achieved great success in some other way were largely helped and led there through reading and mastering many of the greatest books and ideas of history and humankind.

To take it a step further, one of the surest ways to increase your own ability to effect change and really achieve personal excellence in whatever field you've chosen as your life's work is to start reading and listening to important audios today.

Chris Brady put it like this:

> *Are you called to leadership? Are you stirred to effect some great change? Are you dreaming of a vision of a brighter future? Are you inspired to attack the status quo? Take some age-old advice to take some age-old advice. Become an intentional, enthusiastic, consistent, hungry, determined reader, and the result, inevitably, is that you'll become a leader.*

Understanding this fact firmly places reading in the category of "vital behaviors" when it comes to accomplishing your highest goals of success and making a truly meaningful contribution to the world. And once it makes that list, we want to make it *fun* so it'll really get *done*.

For some people, the thought of reading is already an extremely fun idea—nothing sounds better than a good book. Unfortunately, for many others, there is a different sentiment attached.

For those of you who are still wondering why there's a chapter called "Reading" in a book about fun, let's talk about how reading the right things in the right ways and at the right times can be one of the most gloriously fun aspects of your entire life—a project you look forward to and can't wait to get back to whenever anything else interrupts.

## Read Fun Books

The easiest way to start to make reading fun in your life is to simply read fun books. And despite what you're probably thinking, that doesn't mean you have to pick books that will be a waste of your time.

There are all sorts of books out there—from all genres, styles, and types—that have the power to teach you important lessons in ways that nothing else really can.

The habit itself is what matters at first. Then as you read more and more, your taste for the truly excellent will grow, and you will naturally move from the less great books to the greats. But you have to read to do this!

So go the library, the bookstore, or your phone's Kindle app, pick something out, and start reading. Or get great audios that teach important lessons, principles, and skills, and start listening often. The combination of reading and listening is the most effective

> Go the library, the bookstore, or your phone's Kindle app, pick something out, and start reading.

and most fun way to make your learning soar. And make no mistake: learning is fun!

Since the goal here really is twofold (fun *and* growth), and both aspects matter a lot, it's okay if you prioritize one over the other for the moment. As you get deeper into the process, you'll naturally start to seek out both.

Now it's important to note that if you're consistently seeking out and devouring things that are actually *trashy*, this doesn't work the same.

With generally wholesome material, even if it's not the best quality, you'll be training yourself to want better and better quality, and your reading taste and judgment will naturally improve. But when you get the really lame stuff—such as trashy romance novels and the like— you'll actually end up on the opposite spiral: consistently wanting worse and worse.

Basically, the point here is that you shouldn't shut off your judgment or quality meter entirely when you go to pick a book. If you don't find Plato and Aristotle completely riveting at first, you shouldn't start with them, but don't start with stuff you'd honestly have to label as "junk."

We recommend that you find a good book club, or better still a book and audio club, that will send you great reading and listening materials each month. This gives you the benefit of receiving top books and audios selected by knowledgeable experts, month after month.

In fact, the best such club we know of can be found at lifeleadership.com.*

So go pick out a book! Make it fun but worth your time. Then get to reading, and don't stop! Push yourself to try

---

* LIFE Leadership offers several such book and audio subscriptions. Simply click on "Subscriptions" on the main menu to see the available options.

new things. Create a personal competition to see how fast you can get into deeper and higher-quality content. If you persist, this will add a great deal of fun to your life.

### Read to Your Kids

Another excellent way of learning to enjoy reading, which also helps build better relationships and a truly powerful legacy, is to set some time aside to read to your children.

While they're young, this might mean half an hour twice a week when you take them on your lap and read three or four Dr. Seuss books or other family favorites.

As they get older, you'll start to read a chapter here and there from longer books, which you'll finish after a few weeks or months of shared anticipation, excitement, and engagement in the characters, stories, and themes.

When they're ready, it becomes immensely beneficial and lots of fun to have everyone read a book or article on their own and then discuss it as a family.

> Reading together is a blessing to family life in countless ways. It helps everyone keep up on the habit of consistent reading, making it fun and recreational at the same time.

Whatever level of readiness your family is at, reading together is a blessing to family life in countless ways. It helps everyone keep up on the habit of consistent reading, making it fun and recreational at the same time. And as many top educators have taught, reading to children at a young age helps them to better love and better *understand* hard-to-read books later in life.[2]

What a legacy to pass on to your children! Not to mention the family bonding, personal growth, and overall fun you'll experience in the process!

So make this happen. You might not have much time in your week to dedicate to it, but you could find some or make some if you made it a priority. Even if you only read to the family for ten or fifteen minutes here and there throughout the week, it will make a huge difference for everyone involved.

Make it a priority, and you will never regret it. This is so worth it and so much fun!

For example, Chris Brady tells the story of how his wife, Terri, reads *The Best Christmas Pageant Ever* aloud to the whole family each holiday season. Everyone laughs at the voices she uses for each of the characters, and they particularly love her voice for Imogene Herdman.

This is great family fun and has become a tradition of family togetherness. If you already have such traditions, make sure to give them your full focus when it's time. If not, start some. Family traditions can be extremely fun.

### Read for Answers to Tough Questions

One thing we've noticed about life is that tasks that aren't usually our favorites seem a lot more exciting when we can clearly see how they benefit us in important ways.

The way to make your reading do this for you is quite simple: Always read for a purpose! Even if you're reading during leisure time or just for fun, you can always be looking for answers to the tough questions or challenges you're facing, finding bits and pieces from disparate sources to help you in life.

> Even if you're reading during leisure time or just for fun, you can always be looking for answers to the tough questions or challenges you're facing.

The book *Turn the Page* says, "Reading a variety of books to answer big questions helps readers receive fuller and deeper answers, and reading to answer specific questions allows them to learn expressly needed lessons and achieve success in particular areas."

This is a simple task, but as you do it, you will find a lot of success in your reading. Finding the right answers from your reading makes it feel more meaningful, and making it meaningful is a step toward making it fun.

It's pretty easy to notice that when something feels totally meaningless, it usually isn't as enjoyable. We've all seen this in our work and often in school experiences as well. The idea here is to take steps to get more out of reading, which will make it both more valuable as a growth tool and more fun.

So how do you do it? Simple. Just approach each book with a set of questions you're pondering in your life. When you find anything that seems to answer them, pay attention! Take note and act on the inspiration and insights you get from your books. This is deceptively easy, but it will make a big difference in your reading.

Finding the best answers is sometimes as simple as asking the questions in the first place. Once you know what you want to learn, you're going to start finding the answers in what you read. So enjoy!

## Make Reading a Party

Find ways to make reading a celebration or even a party. You can set motivating goals and have exciting competitions with friends to read lots of books or harder ones or to read them faster or more often. This can be great fun. You can also create opportunities to celebrate success and achievement of such goals.

Having parties for those who meet certain challenges with their reading and listening is another fantastic way to keep the magic of reading alive.

Even include a discussion of your readings and audios as part of your day, and that'll make the books themselves more fun, as you get to share your thoughts, feelings, and impressions with others and learn from theirs.

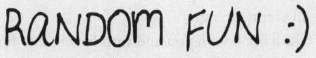

# RANDOM FUN :)

*Just play. Have fun. Enjoy the game.*
~Michael Jordan

Fun parties, competitions, and games make reading a more powerful experience because not only do they get us to read a lot more and enjoy ourselves more in the process, but we also end up learning and growing much more from the experience.

Get creative! Reading is a great excuse to party, play, and compete! It will improve your friendships and increase your life's fun and effectiveness. So what are you waiting for?

**Read on the Go**

Something else you can do to capitalize on the fun powers of reading is to take a book with you wherever you go and use it to fill in already boring moments in your daily routine.

If you're used to spending time waiting for someone and feeling bored anyway, reading a good book instead won't feel like a drag. At the very least, you'll have something to do. And if you're fulfilling goals, winning competitions, and preparing for exciting discussions in the process, or just enjoying what you learn, it will be a no-brainer. Accomplishing things is exhilarating—especially when the alternative is to waste time and *feel* like that's all you're doing!

So take a book with you and turn boring into fun! And listen to audios while you shower, wait, drive, etc. That's easy enough, and it really will make a big difference, both in how much you read and listen and how much time you *don't* waste. Happy reading!

## Reading Will Make All Your Dreams Come True

Remember what Chris Brady said earlier in this chapter? As you become an intentional, enthusiastic, consistent, hungry, and determined reader, you will naturally become a better leader.

And guess what else? You will see your life improve in all sorts of other ways. You will be a better spouse and a better parent. You will be a better mentor and a better listener. You will be better at your work and at your play. You will have more success and *much* more fun.

Reading and listening to audios really is powerful! It can vastly improve and even literally transform your life.

We're all familiar with some version of the Cinderella story—about the girl who worked all day for her evil stepmother and wasn't even allowed to go to the ball.

We know the fairy godmother who came in at the last second and made everything bright and sparkly for the girl. She even got a fancy dress.

Eventually, after continued hardship and difficulty, she had a true rags-to-riches transformation followed by a happily-ever-after life with Prince Charming.

What is less well-known is that in the real world, books can be your fairy godmother! If you want to change your

> In the real world, books can be your fairy godmother! If you want to change your life—make it more fun, more meaningful, and more "happily-ever-after"—start reading!

life—make it more fun, more meaningful, and more "happily-ever-after"—start reading!

Read lots, read well, and read *right*. Listen to audios the same way. As you do, you may even get to stay at the ball past midnight, avoid the inconvenience of losing a shoe, and overcome the risk of having someone else with the exact same shoe size claim to be you—not to mention having your carriage turn back into in a pumpkin!

Reading and listening are magical! You get to experience all sorts of lives and adventures. You get to learn from the world's greatest heroes and leaders. And you get to have some of the world's best fun, without spending money on gas.

## BITE-SIZE FUN

Over 70 percent of public school teachers pay for class supplies with their own money. Go to a local school, ask what supplies a teacher needs, and buy a box of items from the list. Don't break the bank; just do what you can afford. Every little bit will help. Serving others is fun!

## CHAPTER EIGHT

# Vacation

*We are so used to working that not*
*working is the new hard work.*

~Mokokoma Mokhonoana

A good vacation is one of the best ways to have a bunch of great fun, and it's also an important way to apply designed gratification—so that your work stays at its best and you stay at yours.

Chris Brady, author of *A Month of Italy*, truly understands the importance of proper and right vacationing and has dedicated hours of study, research, and thought to helping people come to understand this important principle and more fully apply it in their lives.

*A Month of Italy* is the best book on the topic we've ever seen.

Here are some of his helpful and insightful thoughts on the power, importance, and *fun* of real vacationing:

*The more I've researched the category of vacations, sabbaticals, intentional work breaks, work-fasts, electronic fasts, time off, time out, or whatever else you want to throw into the category, the more I've come into contact with some philosophies that probably never would have made my radar screen. This has been very illuminating, but also a bit disheartening.*

## Why He Wrote the Book

*I set out to write* A Month of Italy: Rediscovering the Art of Vacation *because I felt so entirely blessed to be on my first real sabbatical that I wanted desperately to share what I had learned with others. I had gotten back in touch with a program of maintaining peak performance and razor-sharp clarity of focus.*

*In my own life, I had truly rediscovered the art of vacation. In fact, I came back from that original summer sabbatical so refreshed, so recharged, that within just one year I relocated my family to a different state (a decision with which I'd wrestled for almost a decade), wrote one best-selling book (*Rascal: Making a Difference by Becoming an Original Character*), co-authored another with my good friend Orrin Woodward (*LIFE*), and launched a multimillion-dollar company with seven of my best friends—not bad for a mere four weeks off.*

## His Formula from College

*As I explain in the* Italy *book, I had once possessed a formula that, for me, worked perfectly. It was while I was studying engineering at an intensive undergraduate institute that I had first stumbled across this arrangement.*

*It came from being outgunned and outclassed in almost every way as I struggled with the workload of seven classes per semester and more math and science than I even care to remember. The students around me seemed so much more unconcerned and laid back about it than I did, and, quite frankly, I panicked.*

*They went out to get drunk and I hit the books. I worked so hard I earned the nickname "Machine." My homework was always done on time, I posted very good grades, and I had not an ounce of fun. At least, from Sunday night at about 8:00 until Friday after lunch.*

*In between those times I was a quintessential work-aholic. However (and this is the part where the formula comes in), I would leave campus like a clown shot out of a circus cannon on Friday afternoon and forget all about the place for the weekend.*

*I'd hang out with my girlfriend, visit my parents' cottage in the "up north" of Michigan, and do just about anything except schoolwork. This usually involved all my favorite activities, such as jet skiing, motorcycling in the dunes, playing football with my buddies, water skiing, reading, playing at the beach, and camping.*

*By the time I returned to campus I was clear-headed, wide-eyed, and ready to go. My ambition had been refueled and my tanks refilled.*

## How Had He Lost It?

*I have tried to go back and figure out exactly how or why I lost touch with something that had once been so powerful in my life. The only conclusion I can draw is that I didn't see it as such a stand-alone, creative program at the time.*

*Let's face it; most of us grow up in a school system that sort of takes care of this for us. We are accustomed to summer breaks, holidays, weekends off, and time between level advancements to get mentally ready for the next step.*

*Suddenly, though, we find ourselves out in the "real world" where no hours are off limits when it comes to working a job and vacations are scarce (especially for the new hire).*

*A sort of sick ambition sets in as the aggressiveness of youth pairs itself with the resiliency of youth, blending to obscure the fact that we are not machines and that we need regular "down times" to maximize the "up times."*

*The older we get the less we can get away with recklessly abusing our schedule as though endless effort will somehow produce better results. It can't. In short, I had achieved a lot in my adult life, but I had gotten away from a formula of intentional rest and restoration which could have helped me accomplish so much more.*

*Stephen Covey calls it "sharpening the saw,"[1] and of all his* 7 Habits of Highly Effective People, *it has to be the most neglected. There are scores of books on goal setting, beginning with the end in mind, persevering, and game planning, but almost nobody talks about strategic breaks.*

*It seems that rats in a race are not allowed a pit stop.*

## Is Vacation the End Goal?

*This brings me to some philosophies of happiness which have gathered a following. Certain of these trains of thought suggest that time off is not merely an elixir to heal the wounds of stress and enable one to pursue his or her true calling in life, but rather that time off is the overall point.*

*It's the old pursuit of happiness trap whereby pleasure is sold as fulfillment. "Just do what makes you happy and fill the space in between with enough work to pay for it." "The more you play, the happier you'll be."*

*To me, it's like the old bumper sticker that says, "He who dies with the most toys, wins!" except it's been modified for our twenty-first century sensibilities to nothing more than "He who dies with the most adventures wins!" The new version is just as much of a lie as the older.*

## Don't Get Me Wrong

*On the other hand, however, I am not advocating the workaholism that several generations of Americans have thoroughly proven as the path to ruined health, ruined relationships, and yes, unhappiness.*

*All I'm saying is that we can't swing the pendulum too far the other way. If we're not careful, being idle can easily become an idol in our lives. We slide down the slippery slope of wanting too much of a good thing.*

## Meaninglessness

*Remember: It is not all that important that we succeed,*

> "It is not all that important that we succeed, but it IS supremely important that we matter!"
> ~Chris Brady

*but it IS supremely important that we matter! Wasting our gifts in the pursuit of pleasure is ultimately not fulfilling, and tragically, it keeps us from impacting the lives of others and the world at large.*

*I recently stumbled across this line written by Napoleon Hill toward the end of the Great Depression: "There is something infinitely worse than being forced to work. It is being forced not to work."*

*When we are deprived of meaningful work, either by outside economics (as in Hill's time), or by internalizing incorrect philosophies of "happiness through self-indulgence" (as in our time), we become sick with a sense of emptiness no amount of entertainment can disguise.*

*Deep down, we know we were built for something greater than ourselves.*

### Fulfillment

*We must work in a useful service to truly be fulfilled. True happiness comes from being in line with our God-given calling in life, living consistently with that calling every day, and serving others with every fiber of our being.*

*As I've said elsewhere, the only way to BE happy is to GIVE happy.*

### Sabbatical versus Self-Indulgence

*So there is a significant difference between a strategic sabbatical and self-indulgence. It is this distinction that I strove to demonstrate in* A Month of Italy.

*This is not double talk; it's doubling down on your effectiveness. Oh yeah, and it will be a total blast! Whoever said purpose wasn't fun couldn't have said that on purpose!*

> "Whoever said purpose wasn't fun couldn't have said that on purpose!"
> ~Chris Brady

*So, you probably need a break. But you need it at the right time, in the right way, and for the right reasons.*

### Less and Less from More and More

*Although almost everyone will readily agree that taking effective breaks and time off is necessary, fewer and fewer Americans seem to be doing so. In fact, the United States ranks toward the bottom when compared to other developed countries when it comes to the average number of paid vacation days taken per year.*

*The following chart comes from infoplease.com:*

| | |
|---|---|
| Italy | 42 days |
| France | 37 days |
| Germany | 35 days |
| Brazil | 34 days |
| United Kingdom | 28 days |
| Canada | 26 days |
| Korea | 25 days |
| Japan | 25 days |
| United States | 13 days |

*This disparity is eye-opening. But this is not the only statistic. According to Don Monkerud of AlterNet, "Compared to people in other developed countries, Americans don't ask for more vacation time, don't take all the vacation time their employers give them, and continue to work while they are on vacation." Monkerud's statement is supported by the data.*

*It seems that one third of Americans don't take their allotted vacation time, 37% never take more than a week at a time, only 14% take more than two weeks at a time, and one third of all women and one quarter of all men receive no paid vacations at all.*

*Compare this to the fact that 40% of Americans are now working 50 hours a week, and even when a vacation of sorts is wrangled from the schedule, 88% of Americans* carry electronic devices while away to communicate with work!

According to the Center for Economic Policy and Research, 25% of Americans and 31% of low wage earners get no vacation at all anymore.

Careerbuilder.com stated that "While 84% of workers planned to take at least some time off this year, 32% were taking 5 days or less, and 1 out of 10 were limiting themselves to a long weekend."

In a survey posted on Expedia.com it was estimated that workers would give back to their employers more than 574 million unused vacation days (in the year 2006). That represents nearly two days for every person in the country!

## It All Adds Up to a Tearing Down

What effect does all this work and the corresponding lack of proper breaks have on lifestyle and health? According to the US Centers for Disease Control, "83% of all deaths for adults between 21 and 65 are related to lifestyle."

Joe Robinson, a work-life balance expert and author, stated that "Vacations are theoretical concepts that exist today only on paper. We're supposed to be a nation of fair play; we're a nation of no play." AlterNet

> "Vacations are theoretical concepts that exist today only on paper. We're supposed to be a nation of fair play; we're a nation of no play."
> ~Joe Robinson

reports that one in three US workers report job stress, and those making over $50,000 per year report the highest levels of stress.

And how about retirement? Perhaps we can just count on resting up then. Nope. For the first time in US history, there are four generations in the workplace at the same time, which means people are waiting longer and longer to retire, if ever.

## "But I Know All about Vacations"

"I already take vacations," you may be saying, and that's fantastic, although, as we've just seen, you are among the rare individuals who do.

But mere vacations are not exactly what we are concerned about when discussing the concept of Strategic Sabbaticals. Because, even though people are taking less and less vacations, there is another trend that is part of that: they are taking worse and worse vacations.

What does this mean? It means that there is a right and a not-so-right way to take time off. In other words, there is a difference between rest and restoration.

> "There is a difference between rest and restoration."
> ~Chris Brady

A true vacation should not only be fun, or a chance to get away, but should also rebuild you and spit you back out stronger and better than new.

Too many times vacations resemble the frenzied work life—it's all hurry and scurry to cram in as much "fun" *as possible before the time runs out. Many participants in such vacations find themselves needing a vacation just to rest up from their vacation!*

### "But I Can't *Afford* to Take Time Off!"

*One of the natural responses to the idea of taking breaks, vacations, sabbaticals, or whatever is, "But I can't afford it!" I totally understand this reaction, and I wish to attack this obstacle in a way that, I hope, allows readers to understand that they can figure out a way.*

*Also, I am inclined to believe that when people read A Month of Italy, they will also want to figure out a way!*

*And certainly, it doesn't have to be Italy. A restorative break could occur right at home. The important thing to understand is that money is not able to hold you back from doing what you really want (and need) to do—unless you let it!*

*The current economic climate has been hard on people, and I in no way want to make light of that fact, nor discount the pressure one feels when experiencing financial hardship.*

*There is no pressure quite like financial pressure. However, there are always options if one thinks hard enough and has the right attitude about money.*

*It is important to establish right up front that arranging for the financial means to take restorative breaks in one's life should be a priority.*

*There is no reason that a budget should not include some money to allow one to take the breaks needed to accomplish a little rest and, more importantly, resto-ration. It's a matter of prioritization.*

*In our materialistic culture we are sold the lie that more and more stuff will bring happiness and fulfillment. It simply isn't true.*

*The other fallacy is that people actually believe they "can't afford it." But studies show that people who complain of having no money still manage to possess expensive smart phones, automobiles, air conditioning, cable or satellite television, video games, designer purses, large wardrobes of clothes, and any number of other things that cannot by any stretch of the imagination be considered necessary for living.*

*The truth of the matter is that we've been conditioned by our materialistic society to have a lot of stuff we really don't need. And in most cases, when people feel they "can't" afford a break, it's because they have become deeply indebted from purchasing stuff they really didn't need with money they hadn't yet earned.*

*As we've been discussing, one thing we do need, however, is proper downtime. It's a pity that we trade our limited resources for material items that don't bring health and well-being but then claim we*

> "It's a pity that we trade our limited resources for material items that don't bring health and well-being but then claim we can't afford to take time off which is *proven* to enhance our health and well-being."
> ~Chris Brady

can't afford to take time off which is **proven** to enhance our health and well-being.

We've simply got our priorities out of whack.

Slow down the materialism consumption machine a little bit and free up some funds for more essential aspects of living—such as restorative breaks.

Use the many tools available today to generate a budget that makes provision for less spending in order to pay for strategic breaks.

Be creative with your strategic breaks so they aren't that expensive. After all, how much does it (or should it) cost to unwind? There are many free ways to decompress. Sell your unnecessary material items and put the money into time off.

And ultimately, use the renewed vigor and clarity you'll get from proper, strategic sabbaticals (both large and small) to get better and better at what you do and increase your earning power.

Pairing this with increased discipline in handling your money will go a long way toward creating a "productive spiral" of higher reward for better performance because of proper time off.

It's not a pipe dream; it can be a reality.

And I promise you it's worth it!

# BITE-SIZE FUN

Pull your kids together, or some friends, and tell them the funniest story from your life. Ask them to do the same.

CHAPTER NINE

# Family

*Family is not an important thing;*
*it's everything.*

~MICHAEL J. FOX

**M**ost of us can agree that spending time with family
should be a priority in our lives. Unfortunately, it's
also one that many people find easier to ignore than most
others.

In short, while we all think we should spend more time
with our families, we too often let this need slide in favor
of something that seems more urgent at the moment.

This is actually tragic in a number of ways. To begin
with, we have the obvious
negatives of not properly
attending to family needs and
relationships.

When we don't correctly
support and strengthen these
vital relationships, they're

> While we all think
> we should spend
> more time with our
> families, we too
> often let this need
> slide in favor of
> something that
> seems more urgent.

bound to suffer—particularly in ways that hurt other areas of our lives.

## The Spirit of "And"

The book *Mentoring Matters*[1] from the LIFE Leadership Essentials Series teaches the power and importance of what it calls "the Spirit of 'And.'" Here's what it says:

> *In knowing which details matter, as well as which can be disregarded, and then giving the details the attention they deserve, leaders are actually improving their ability to effectively focus.*
>
> *Of course your mentee wants to be successful in business, and he will find more success by taking care of business and family and service and other important things rather than ignoring important things and only working on his career.*

The book goes on to explain that you will be more effective in *every* aspect of your life if you make sure to properly prioritize and strengthen *each* aspect. In other words, you will be a better businessperson if you're a good businessperson *and* a good parent. You'll be a better parent if you're a good parent *and* a good spouse. And you'll be a better spouse if you're a good spouse *and* a good community member. And so on.

> You will be a better businessperson if you're a good businessperson *and* a good parent.

In short, there are many parts of your life that matter, and as you give each the right energy and effort, you will see all the others improve in powerful ways.

Likewise, when you *don't* give attention to the different areas of life that really matter, that failure bleeds into other areas of life, and they begin to suffer. This drains the fun out of life.

## Let's Talk Family

Now that we understand this important principle, it's time to talk about its application to family. We know that family is one of the significant parts of our lives that really deserves and needs our attention.

Failing to give that attention is going to make your efforts in other areas less valuable. But properly attending to it will make the work you're already doing go way further. Knowing that should help you make family a priority.

We're not saying you should drop everything else that matters and spend every moment following your kids around like a protective guard dog or even a devoted puppy. Obviously that would not help matters in the spirit of "and."

We're just saying you should *actually* make them the priority you've always known they should be. Find out what the right balance is, and dedicate yourself to following it.

> Find out what the right balance is, and dedicate yourself to following it.

And guess what? There's a reason this topic is being discussed in a book about fun.

*Not* following through on your ever-repeated goal to "spend more time with family" makes you miss out on tons of really incredible, wholesome, life-changing fun. And who'd want to miss out on that?

## Get to Know Your Family Better

As you spend more time with your family—the right amount at the right times and in the right ways—you'll start to know them in new and deeper ways. Sometimes it will take lots of work, but as you really make time to build those relationships and get to know your family, you will find a whole new set of incredible friends!

Let's be clear about something: You're going to find out

> Enjoy the eccentricities of your family.

just how unique and strange and amusing your family is. What fun! Seriously. How wholesome and enjoyable! As Claire LaZebnik put it, "No one's family is normal. Normalcy is a lie invented by advertising agencies to make the rest of us feel inferior."[2] So enjoy the eccentricities of your family; have fun with them!

You'll also learn, more every day, how amazing every individual member of your family is—how much potential greatness they all have within.

Getting to know your family will bring on plenty of smiles, laughs, and fun. Enjoy the experience! This is something you owe yourself. It's also something you'll never regret; it's *that* worth it!

## Play as a Family

Call your family together. Spend the evening playing games. If it's warm outside, maybe throw around a ball. If not, pull out your favorite board or card games and make a night of it.

Perhaps your family would enjoy a scavenger hunt around town. Split into two teams, and get on it!

Whatever you choose, make a point of planning creative and exciting activities for your family to do together. Even consider dedicating a night or two each week to this, and let the games begin!

These nights will be some of the most fun in your entire week. They will also help your family feel loved and taken care of at a whole new level. Victor Hugo said, "The supreme happiness in life is the conviction that we are loved."

One of the surest ways to achieve this in your family is to let them see you dropping everything else and just playing with them. Remember, your family spells love T-I-M-E.

Turn your phone off, put your computer away, and be there with your family. It's going to be loads of fun, and it will make you more effective at the rest of your week's tasks. Just as the right kind of vacation brings powerful renewal, as Chris Brady discussed, the right kind of family time makes you much better in every facet of life!

Dr. Seuss described this balanced mentality thus: "When he worked, he really worked. But when he played, he really PLAYED." It's so important to live this way if you want to have a fun and successful life—especially when it comes to your family.

> "When he worked,
> he really worked.
> But when he played,
> he really PLAYED."
> ~Dr. Seuss

So play with your family! And when you do, *really* play. Be there with them, and enjoy it. This will make it easier for you to be wherever else you need to be when you need to be there. You'll have more fun, your family will feel more loved, and your whole life will greatly benefit.

## Work as a Family

Along with the projects and activities you do with your family that are dedicated to fun, you should also dedicate time to working together.

> Working together
> as a family is a
> great source of fun,
> a powerful way to
> bond, and a vitally
> important learning
> experience for
> children of all ages.

Take everyone outside for an hour of yard work, or gather in the kitchen to let Mom off her feet after a long day.

Whether raking leaves or preparing dinner, working together as a family is a great source of fun, a powerful way to bond, and a vitally important learning experience for children of all ages.

And family projects are an excellent way to help children *feel* the fun of it all.

This is an important way to teach children how to work and how to truly *enjoy* work. Make it different from their normal chores and household responsibilities.

This is a time for you to actually dig in side by side with your children, rather than just assigning them tasks and waiting for them to report. This latter method can be valuable and important in some circum-stances, but you should also

> Make a point of saying *"Let's* work" sometimes, not just *"Go* work."

make a point of saying *"Let's* work" sometimes, not just *"Go* work."[3]

Working together is great for a family! Getting everyone involved makes it fun, and as you also make a point of learning from these shared experiences, you'll be creating a better family culture and stronger family togetherness.

Everyone will enjoy themselves.

### Learn as a Family

As you work and play together, making everything fun, you should also make a point of turning these activities into fantastic learning experiences.

As you work together, pull everyone aside and take a moment to discuss and debrief. Share lessons and examples you witnessed from your children and their interactions.

If you're watching as you work and play together, we're sure you'll observe things that could be beneficial lessons for your children—but only if they *see* them. So point them out! Help your children notice the lessons surrounding them. It's simple, once you see them, to take a moment and mention them to your family members. Open a discussion and ask each person what lessons or examples he or she saw. Keep it going. Everyone can learn a lot.

Again, it's easy for you to add a little debriefing for learning at the end of any family project, and it makes it much more valuable. It also increases the fun, if done right.

In fact, doing this will actually make *you* more likely to notice and learn from these activities yourself. So watch and learn, and help your family do the same.

And don't forget that in addition to working and playing together, reading is another great way to learn together.

## Learn *from* Your Family

William Saroyan said, "While we try to teach our children all about life, our children teach us what life is all about." This statement brings up a fantastic principle of both the fun and the power associated with family.

> "While we try to teach our children all about life, our children teach us what life is all about."
> ~William Saroyan

Learning to have fun in the simple and easygoing ways of children will make an enormous difference in your ability to enjoy the little things and find pleasure in the most basic experiences.

As you spend more and more time with your children, especially when they're young, you'll find yourself constantly learning important lessons to apply to other areas of life.

Bestselling author Oliver DeMille teaches that everyone you ever meet has some deep and important genius within. This applies to your family— even the youngest members.

> As you spend more and more time with your children, especially when they're young, you'll find yourself constantly learning important lessons to apply to other areas of life.

Use family fun times to help you prepare to better accomplish your mission in life. This is both enjoyable and just plain smart. If you're going to have little geniuses around you all the time, you may as well take notes.

## Sacrifice as a Family

Learning to sacrifice together is another powerful and important lesson that will benefit your family greatly.

To begin with, if you help your spouse and children understand your unique life purpose and why it's so important to you and ask them to support you in your hard work and to sacrifice time along with you, they will be willing and excited to feel like a part of your cause.

When you give them the chance, they'll be thrilled to be a part of your support team, and if you don't, they'll often feel abandoned or ignored by their "workaholic parent."

This kind of communication and understanding really does make all the difference, and it helps everyone make the most of the times you *do* spend together, rather than feeling resentful or bitter about the hard times. So invite them to sacrifice with you for your mission.

And learn to do the same for them.

This will help them understand the importance of pursuing their own mission and properly communicating with their families about it in the future. Doing this emphasizes the value of mission and strengthens family relationships, rather than pulling people apart.

Another important aspect of sacrificing together as a family is finding opportunities to serve and care for others in your community in meaningful ways. This can be fantastic fun!

Giving up some comforts or conveniences for a cause is a great way to raise children of character. Make this a family activity, and sacrifice together! The growth, family togetherness, and fun will amaze you. Also, you'll be giving a meaningful contribution to the world in many different ways.

### Change the World Together!

Mother Teresa said, "The way you help heal the world is you start with your own family." As you make a real effort to strengthen and build your family, you'll be having tons of fun while impacting the world in significant ways.

Teach your family the power of growing together in ways that lead to the betterment of the world as a whole.

With your spouse and children, figure out what your family's mission in the world is, and start working toward it together.

Show your children that they can truly change the world for the better. Jennifer Donnelly said, "Together in our house, in the firelight, we are the world made small."[4]

Creating a family culture of understanding the power of the individual and of the unified family to effect real and lasting change in the world is one of the most incredible experiences you'll ever have in life. It is immensely meaningful and very much worth it. And honestly, it's crazy fun!

So build a phenomenal family. And spend more time with them! Play, work, learn, read, sacrifice, and serve together.

You know you want to, and now we've told you why you've *got* to. And to top it off, it's one of the most beautiful types of fun you'll ever achieve because if you do it right, it will never end.

# BITE-SIZE FUN

Take a sticky note and write a nice message on it for one person in your family. Draw a heart or smiley face at the bottom. Then put it where only that person will see it but where he or she will be sure to find it.

## CHAPTER TEN

# Romance

*It is a truth universally acknowledged, that a single man in*
*possession of a large fortune must be in want of a wife.*

~JANE AUSTEN

O ne of the most potentially fun and fulfilling aspects of
your life is the realm of romance. If you're married,
think back to when you were first wooing your spouse.

Few will argue with the statement that the romantic
pursuits of dating and court-
ship produce some of the most
thrilling and satisfying laughter,
memories, competition, and
fun one can have in life. We
tend to look back on those times
and think, *"Man, we had fun!"*

> When approached
> correctly, romance
> can and will get
> better and better
> as you get
> deeper into it.

Whether the years since
then have made you feel that romance only gets better or
they've made you come to miss the "good old days," we
can all remember having great fun in our early romantic
lives.

For our part, we have come to believe that, when approached correctly, romance can and will get better and better as you get deeper into it. And "better and better" definitely includes a lot of fun.

### Romantic *Pursuit*

If you haven't found your romance to be a source of much fun lately, and even if it has been everything you could wish for, there's a good chance you can help things along by remembering one of the keys that made it fun "way back when."

Before you were many years married, before you were secure in your relationship, before you got lazy and complacent and viewed it all as easy, you looked at your relationship as a pursuit.

On some level, both of you were being your extra-good selves, being creative about making the other person feel taken care of, and doing things to "put in a good word." In short, you were actively pursuing the apple of your eye, the relationship, and his or her good opinion.

In some ways "romantic pursuit" is a state that ends. Having received the favor and hand of your truly beloved, you are no longer in constant and uncertain pursuit. But the pursuit shouldn't end—not ever!

One of the cool things about marriage is that you don't have to feel uncertain about your true love's loyalty or feelings toward you; you know he or she loves you and is committed to staying. However, if you want it all to be fun—in fact, if you want to keep even the certainty and security of commitment—you can't let this sense of secu-rity lead you to stop pursuing the relationship, your spouse's happiness, and the romance of the whole endeavor.

> If you want it all to be fun, you can't let the sense of security lead you to stop pursuing the relationship, your spouse's happiness, and the romance of the whole endeavor.

In this way, romantic pursuit can and should be an active and eternal state. For romance to truly flourish, you have to be constantly seeking and working toward it in real and tangible ways.

You have to make some sacrifices and undertake some difficult tasks to make it really work. You need to brain-storm and plan and do things for your spouse—lots of things. Luckily, when you *do* make romance a daily pursuit, you're likely to succeed and have tons of fun in the process.

## Serve Your Spouse

Whether you have a happy marriage or not, one of the best ways to increase the romance, love, and fun in your relationship is to start more actively and consistently serving your spouse. Specifically, focus on giving service without expecting anything in return.

When you do things for someone expecting a specific response and then feel disappointed or resentful when they don't act accordingly, you're acting in a way that's both unreasonable and damaging to the relationship.

When the other person has no idea what is going on in your mind, and especially when you go to your spouse after the fact and try to demand compensation for your service, it hurts the relationship.

Obviously, this is not what we're suggesting, and it certainly won't make your romance more fun.

> One of the best ways to increase the romance, love, and fun in your relationship is to start more actively and consistently serving your spouse.

It's also not that helpful when you go around doing things *you* really want done, considering that service to your spouse, and then calling it good.

If, on the other hand, you brainstorm actions that would be truly meaningful to your spouse—things *he or she* wants—and then do them without expecting anything back, you will find that, at the very least, your own love and appreciation for your spouse is increased significantly.

You will start to feel more positive in the relationship. It will all be better and more fun—even if it was good to start with.

In addition to brainstorming ways to serve, also just ask your spouse what he or she wants.

Of course, when we say that you should keep up the pursuit, we aren't saying you should have warlike competitions with your spouse. But if you start competing with yourself on how well you can serve and please him or her, you're bound to win at least some of the time!

In most cases—though this is not your reason for serving—your spouse will start to notice what you're doing and start a little service of his or her own.

As you get to a place where both of you are in friendly competition with yourselves to see how each can truly *complete* the other, you're going to find a lot of romance, happiness, and fun in the process.

Benedict Cumberbatch said: "The further you get away from yourself, the more challenging it is. Not to be in your comfort zone is great fun."

As you set a goal to really get outside yourself—to get out of your comfort zone, truly loving, serving, and pleasing your spouse in meaningful ways—you will experience a dramatic increase in the love and happiness in your life. With love and happiness comes romance, and with romance comes fun heaped upon glorious fun.

> As you set a goal to really get outside yourself—to get out of your comfort zone, truly loving, serving, and pleasing your spouse in meaningful ways—you will experience a dramatic increase in the love and happiness in your life.

## Pursue a Purpose

Connecting with your spouse on the core-to-core level of mission and purpose is perhaps the best way to strengthen your efforts toward your biggest dreams and goals. It's also arguably the best way to bond as a couple in deep and meaningful ways. And to top it off, it will be one of the greatest sources of strength and comfort to you in times of difficulty or failure.

Building this aspect of your romance will be fun as you do it and truly priceless when it matters most.

So get together and learn from each other what your purpose is. There will be parts that you spearhead and others you leave to him or her, but there will also be areas where your efforts should intersect and even combine.

> Building the aspect of your romance of connecting on a core-to-core level of mission and purpose will be fun as you do it and truly priceless when it matters most.

Communicating and committing to this project will make you a more effective team and give you lots to talk about on your picnics. Figuring it out will be an exciting adventure, and it really will make the rest of the journey easier and better.

So dig out your biggest basket and a blanket, prepare an outdoor feast, and head for the hills—literally. If you both know you're going on a date but also discussing your mission and purpose, it can be both fun and meaningful.

Communicate, and don't be too strict about your timing. If you end up talking about other things or just being with each other for part of it, let that happen. This is supposed to be fun. But make sure you keep going until you're really clear and unified on your purpose, mission, and dreams. Take weeks or months, if needed, to get this right.

## Dream Build

Another essential endeavor of highly successful couples, which also happens to be tremendously fun, is dream building. Like mission or purpose building, this is where you and your spouse get together and talk about your goals, roles, and future. But this time, the focus is on your dreams rather than how to get them.

What do you want your future to look like? What does success as a couple and as individuals mean to you? What are your hopes, dreams, and ambitions? What do you want to do together for fun? Read together? Go to Italy together? Serve together? What else?

Building dreams together and then working to make them reality is going to add all sorts of enjoyment to your relationship, and it also happens to be the only way to achieve real success. If you don't know what success is, or if you aren't working toward it, you'll never achieve it.

So figure out what matters to you as a couple. Ask yourselves questions, and work out the answers together. Where do you want to be in ten years, and how are you going to get there? What do you want to have? Where do you want to live? What do you want your days to look like? How do you want to be spending your time? Once you know the answers to these questions, what are you going to do to get there?

The process of asking and discussing these questions together can be endlessly fun!

Build dreams together and then work hard to make them happen. This is the path of success, and it's more fun than just about anything else, especially when you're doing it with the person you love.

Start building your castles in the air, so you can start climbing—or constructing, when necessary—the ladder toward them. This is another great picnic discussion, but it also works beside the fireplace with a cup of cocoa.

> Have fun dreaming together about all the fun you're going to have as you make your dreams come true!

Have fun dreaming together about all the fun you're going to have as you make your dreams come true!

## Quality Leisure

While it's incredibly exciting to build missions and dreams together, it's also important to dedicate some time to pure fun and leisure.

You don't want *every* date to be about planning or dreaming, or it'll start to feel like you're always working and never just having fun.

Make sure you take time to just be with each other! Be creative, and do things you really enjoy. Spend most of your leisure time together doing all sorts of interesting activities and sometimes just relaxing in each other's company.

When you're reading, it can be fun to do so in the same room with different books, stopping every now and then to share cool quotes, ideas, or principles you read. Or read the same book. Or listen to an audio together and pause it to discuss what you hear.

Whatever hobbies or leisure activities you develop for your time together, make sure you spend the time! This will be some of the best fun of your life, and it will be an excellent source of renewal for each of you individually and as a couple.

Keep playing together, in various activities and ways, and you'll have plenty of fun! This is an important method of bonding and connecting, and it really will build your romance and your happiness.

**Keep Dating!**

Similar to the idea of spending quality leisure time with each other is the idea of dating forever. But it's important to understand the differences and really do both.

Spending leisure time together can often be informal, undefined, and sometimes infrequent—especially during busy times at work or with the kids. Dating, by contrast, should be a particular activity that you make sure to do quite regularly.

This doesn't mean you have to spend lots of money or make it crazy-fancy, but dating does call for a higher level of commitment and follow-through. It should also be a time where you get a babysitter and take time for just the two of you.

As you make dates a priority in your life and refuse to let them become too few or far between, you'll see your closeness, romance, relationship, and fun increase and improve.

Plan dates in such a way that you can both really *be there*. If you must have the phone in case of an emergency with the kids, fine, but don't let work or other concerns distract you from what you're doing.

> A date is a special occasion specifically dedicated to building the romance and togetherness in your relationship, so make it count.

This is a special occasion specifically dedicated to building the romance and togetherness in your relationship, so make it count. Be romantic in ways your spouse will notice. Understand his or her love language[1] and act accordingly. But most of all, both of you, *have fun!*

**Let the Years Come!**

When you make your romance a constant pursuit, your years will be filled with laughter, happiness, and fun. As you take time to build your relationship together in all areas of your lives, you will be a great help and comfort to each other.

And as you become more fully one—the best team you can be—you will have the deepest and best kind of fun out there. This is the kind that comes with true love, companionship, and happiness.

So start making your romance the fun it is so naturally close to being. Whatever the current state of your relationship, you can elevate it, making it more excellent and enjoyable. As you do, your life will improve dramatically.

You'll be able to look time in the face and say, "Let the years come!"—knowing all the while that every new year brings new adventures and joys for you and your one and only.

Laugh together and hold hands. With this kind of present, the future is full of fun!

## BITE-SIZE FUN

Take a trip together back to the town, school, or place where you first met. If possible, stand in the very spot. Take a walk down memory lane together and see where it leads.

# Becoming Fun Experts

*Live and work but do not forget to play,*
*to have fun in life and really enjoy it.*

~EILEEN CADDY

We started this book with the idea that if we don't have fun in life, family, and work, then these things aren't much fun. This is actually a very profound statement. The solution, of course, is to have more fun.

We've covered a number of ways to do this, and each of them has great potential to significantly improve our lives, infuse them with more fun, and simultaneously add to our success and happiness. Besides all these benefits, having more fun usually has a direct, positive impact on our most important relationships.

> Having more fun usually has a direct, positive impact on our most important relationships.

But there is a second step beyond this first one of finding more fun in life. And that is to attune our mind, ears, and eyes to fun. We should recognize opportunities for fun.

We should become a human fun radar, always noticing when fun is possible.

## Human Fun Radar

We don't have to jump at every opportunity for fun. But we do need to be the kind of people who at least pick up on such favorable circumstances. This allows us to choose fun when we want more of it and to help others do the same.

For example, Chris Brady listed the following ways to notice and have more fun in life:

1. *Change your routine.*
2. *Do something new.*
3. *Meet someone new.*
4. *Get reacquainted with someone from your past.*
5. *Create something.*
6. *Play a harmless prank.*
7. *Make a fool of yourself. (It's very important to be able to handle this well, and once you can, it'll be tons of fun.)*
8. *Scavenger hunt.*
9. *Rearrange something in your surroundings.*
10. *Eat meals at the wrong times.*
11. *Read a lighthearted book.*
12. *Watch a comedy movie with others.*
13. *Answer questions in an unexpected way to get a reaction or catch someone off guard.*

14. *Play Legos. (You might be surprised how much fun this is!)*
15. *Write a sarcastic poem.*
16. *Dream build.*
17. *Plan a surprise for someone.*
18. *Find something to celebrate, and do it.*
19. *Start a brand-new family tradition.*
20. *Come up with nicknames for everyone (not negative ones).*
21. *Go somewhere new.*
22. *Go dark (shut off and get away from all electronics for a period of time).*
23. *Do a mad-lib-type story with your kids.*

This list could go on and on. For example, try the following:

## BITE-SIZE FUN

Next time you see a rainbow, stop whatever you are doing and just watch it for at least fifteen minutes (or until it disappears). If you are driving, pull over first. Pay attention to how beautiful the rainbow is. Notice every color. Keep watching, and see what feelings come.

## BITE-SIZE FUN

Take an afternoon to go to pawn shops, thrift stores, and yard sales looking for an old, inexpensive pocket watch—you know, the kind your grandpa or great-grandpa probably wore.

:)

## BITE-SIZE FUN

If you are on Facebook, change your account settings for language to "English (Pirate)."

:)

In his book *A Whole New Mind*,[1] bestselling author Daniel Pink, tells the story of a group in India who started a Laughing Club at work. They set a specific time to meet each day and share funny experiences and stories—but most of all, to laugh!

Pink goes on to tell how much this increased their productivity and effectiveness at their work as well as their overall fun and happiness. Consider who *you* should start a laughing club with!

In the book *The Happiness Advantage*,[2] author Shawn Achor takes on the commonly believed idea that hard work = success = happiness. Instead, he teaches that bringing happiness—through fun—into the hard work from stage one is actually a necessary step to achieving the truest and best success.

If you try to save up "happiness time" for the end of the work, the work might never get done, and it almost certainly won't get done as well. By including happiness in the hard work—finding ways to make work fun and rewarding— you'll actually increase your ability to work hard, along with the effectiveness of that hard work. This is where true success comes from.

> By including happiness in the hard work—finding ways to make work fun and rewarding—you'll actually increase your ability to work hard, along with the effectiveness of that hard work.

Those who are truly successful understand the importance of combining both happiness *and* accomplishment.

## Be the Fun

These principles and pursuits can help you become more attuned to the fun around you and quicker to note opportunities to increase the fun. As you do, fun will follow you, and people will come to associate you with the fun to be found in various facets of life.

Here are some important side effects of being an overall fun person:

1. Fun helps attitude (yours and everyone else's).
2. Your fun and fun attitude break down barriers.
3. Fun builds trust.
4. Fun makes people like you.
5. Fun creates memories and shared experiences.
6. Fun allows for increased truth sharing (by adding sugar with the medicine).

All of these naturally increase your effectiveness and improve your leadership as well as the quality of your relationships, success, and personal happiness.

## Apply and Accomplish

We've said it time and again, but it's a significant point to remember: you'll accomplish way more in life if you learn to make it fun.

Here are some additional areas to consider making more fun:

**Advertising:** There are a few excellent illustrations of the power of fun applied to advertising to be found in the realm of insurance commercials. Specifically, Geico has had a number of highly successful TV ad campaigns because they've made a name for themselves with entertaining advertisements that people who'd normally skip past all commercials will stop to watch.

It's easy to remember the commercial that asked "Could switching to Geico really save you 15 percent or more on car insurance?—Did the Little Piggy cry 'Weeweewee,' all the way home?" Or what about the "so easy a caveman could do it" commercial? And Allstate has also had a lot of success with its "Avoid mayhem, like me" commercials.

Whether you end up buying what they offer or not, some people do—because they actually watched the commercials. And they watched them because it was more fun than just skipping them.

**Writing and blogging:** It's pretty easy to find examples of this out there. Consider bloggers and writers who use fun titles or quotations to spice up their work or make jokes and tell funny stories to illustrate their points.

For example, consider how the book *Financial Fitness* quotes Jarod Kintz:

> *I think the key indicator for wealth is not good grades, work ethic, or IQ. I believe it's*

*relationships. Ask yourself two questions: How many people do I know, and how much ransom money could I get for each one?*[3]

This definitely adds a laugh to the experience, in a way that keeps you excited and interested in the important principles and techniques the book is teaching.

**Sermons**: The topic and message of sermons are often deep and serious, but having an audience that's engaged and *happy* is a very positive thing. You've heard the saying, "Much truth is said in jest," and it has some powerful application here.

By using humor and fun in your sermons, you create a bond with your audience that helps them feel comfortable and safe. Once you've created this environment, you can expect them to be a lot more willing and ready to listen and apply what you have to say about difficult changes necessary to truly improve their lives.

**Public speaking:** If you've ever witnessed a speech where the speaker understood how to effectively include fun and laughter, you know why this is good. Think back to that speaker and how his or her way of making things fun actually made you listen *better.*

In contrast, most of you have also been to a speech or presentation where the person talking managed to bore you out of your mind. How well did you listen?

How much of the message presented did you really apply in your life? The book *SPLASH!*[4] from the LIFE Leadership Essentials Series has a lot to add on this subject and can help you learn the most effective ways to make your speeches more engaging and fun so they profoundly impact the audience.

**Business communications and e-mails/texts**: Doug Lipp wrote in *Disney U* about how the Disney company intentionally uses humor in its communications and employee relations. In fact, they were probably the first to use humor to leaven such mundane outlets as the employee handbook or rulebook.

Making these kinds of materials humorous and fun for people ensures that people give them more attention and energy than they might otherwise. When you have something important to get done—especially when it's something that might seem boring or mundane—incorporating humor and fun is a powerful way to make it happen in the most efficient and effective ways.

**Funerals**: You have to be extremely careful and tasteful about adding fun to funerals because you can really hurt feelings and cause great offense if you're not. But when it's done right, it can be very powerful. One example of this is a story Chris Brady told about one of his friends:

*Tony is the funniest man I've ever hung around.*
*He is never more than three sentences away from*

*a joke or pun or funny quip. Apparently this man,*
*who was a lifelong friend of Tony's, would always*
*say, "Tony, I'm going to have you get up and tell*
*a joke at my funeral!"*

*Which actually happened just last year.*
*Apparently Tony got up and related that story,*
*told of their long relationship and how it was*
*founded on humor, and then told some of the*
*deceased person's most favorite jokes.*

In this situation, because it was done correctly, the jokes were perfect. The family and loved ones enjoyed them deeply, and the whole mood was lightened in a positive way.

**Facial Expressions**: Most people underestimate the power and importance of a smile. Likewise, most people think they smile most of the time, while very few actually do. Make a point of smiling more, and you'll have more fun and be a better influence on those around you.

> Most people underestimate the power and importance of a smile.

## Step Up the Fun

There are many other ways to use fun to improve life and work. Again, the first step to a fun life is to add more fun. The second is to become a fun "expert," always looking for ways to make things more fun and remaining attuned to possible fun options in any endeavor, task, group, etc.

It is almost impossible to have too much fun in life because real fun is the natural result of applying solid principles and living a successful and meaningful life. The best leaders have a great deal of fun because success and fun come from the same origin: applying true principles in the right way at the right time.

People who only do this to get the job done, however, miss out on the beauty and joy of the journey. Those who have fun along the way, not as an excuse to shirk their potential but as a natural part of becoming their best, actually reach the highest goals and achievements.

> The best leaders have a great deal of fun because success and fun come from the same origin: applying true principles in the right way at the right time.

Fun makes success more attainable, and it makes the journey more exciting, enjoyable, and excellent. This is the power of fun. And make no mistake: Fun (or the lack of it) has an incredible amount of power in our lives. In truth, fun is power. The key for leaders is to access and leverage this power in a way that makes a real difference!

> Fun makes success more attainable, and it makes the journey more exciting, enjoyable, and excellent.

As you learn how to do this and, most important, make it a central habit in your life, you will experience some of the best fun ever.

So start today. Turn on your human fun radar, and start thinking about the kind of designed gratification that will profoundly bless your whole life.

Dr. Seuss famously wrote: "When you're in a slump, you're not in for much fun. Un-slumping yourself is not easily done." But it doesn't have to be this way. Great fun is as easy as the many options covered in this book. Choose fun, and take action.

Make your life more fun. Lighten up, get a life, and improve your relationships, leadership skills, and level of happiness—all by tapping into the power of fun!

# RANDOM FUN :)

*Today was good. Today was fun.*
*Tomorrow is another one.*
~Dr. Seuss

# NOTES

## Prologue

1. Orrin Woodward, "Thrill of Victory, Agony of Defeat, and Joy of Learning." Blog post from August 24, 2013, orrinwoodwardblog.com/2013/08/24/thrill-of-victory-agony-of-defeat-joy-of-learning/.

## Introduction

1. Thomas Paine, "The Crisis No. I," *The American Crisis*, December 23, 1776.

2. Shawn Achor, *The Happiness Advantage: The Seven Principles of Positive Psychology That Fuel Success and Performance at Work* (New York: Crown Business, 2010), 50–53.

## Chapter 1

1. Stephen King, *Hearts in Atlantis* (New York: Scribner, 1999).

2. Phil Callaway, *Making Life Rich Without Any Money* (Eugene, OR: Harvest House Publishers, 1998).

## Chapter 2

1. Lorii Myers, 3 Off the Tee: *Make It Happen: A Healthy, Competitive Approach to Achieving Personal Success* (Barrie, ON, Canada: ii leda Publishing Corp., 2012).

2. Orrin Woodward and Oliver DeMille, *LeaderShift: A Call for Americans to Finally Stand Up and Lead* (New York: Hachette Book Group, 2013).

3. James J. Freeland, Daniel J. Lathrope, Stephen A. Lind, and Richard B. Stephens, *Fundamentals of Federal Income Taxation: Cases and Materials*, 16th Edition, University Casebooks (Foundation Press, 2011).

## Chapter 5

1. Rick Hanson, Ph.D., *Hardwiring Happiness: The New Brain Science of Contentment, Calm, and Confidence* (New York: Harmony, 2013).

**Chapter 6**

1  "Lookin' for Love," *Urban Cowboy* soundtrack, written by Wanda Mallette, Bob Morrison, and Patti Ryan, performed by Johnny Lee, produced by John Boylan, Full Moon label, released June 30, 1980.

2  Chris Brady, *A Month of Italy: Rediscovering the Art of Vacation* (Flint, MI: Obstaclés Press, 2012).

**Chapter 7**

1  LIFE Leadership Essentials Series, *Turn the Page: How to Read Like a Top Leader* (Flint, MI: Obstaclés Press, 2014).

2  Oliver and Rachel DeMille, *Leadership Education: The Phases of Learning*, Third Edition (Cedar City, UT: TJEd.org, 2013).

**Chapter 8**

1  Steven Covey, *The 7 Habits of Highly Effective People* (New York: Simon & Schuster, 1989).

**Chapter 9**

1  LIFE Leadership Essentials Series, *Mentoring Matters: Targets, Techniques, and Tools for Becoming a Great Mentor* (Flint, MI: Obstaclés Press, 2013).

2  Claire LaZebnik, *Epic Fail* (New York: HarperTeen, 2011).

3  Oliver DeMille, *A Thomas Jefferson Education: Teaching a Generation of Leaders for the Twenty-First Century* (Cedar City, UT: George Wythe College Press, 2006).

4  Jennifer Donnelly, *Revolution* (New York: Delacorte Press, 2010), 24.

**Chapter 10**

1  Gary Chapman, *The Five Love Languages: The Secret to Love that Lasts* (Chicago: Northfield Publishing, 1992).

**Conclusion**

1  Daniel Pink, A *Whole New Mind: Why Right-Brainers Will Rule the Future* (New York: Penguin Group, 2005).

2  Shawn Achor, *The Happiness Advantage: The Seven Principles of Positive Psychology That Fuels Success and Performance at Work* (New York: Crown Business, 2010).

3  LIFE Leadership Essentials Series, *Financial Fitness: The Offense, Defense, and Playing Field of Personal Finance* (Flint, MI: Obstaclés Press, 2013).

4  LIFE Leadership Essentials Series, *SPLASH!: A Leader's Guide to Effective Public Speaking* (Flint, MI: Obstaclés Press, 2014).

# Other Books in the
# LIFE Leadership Essentials Series

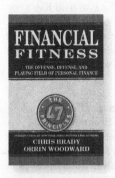

*Financial Fitness: The Offense, Defense, and Playing Field of Personal Finance* with Introduction by Chris Brady and Orrin Woodward – $21.95

If you ever feel that you're too far behind and can't envision a better financial picture, you are so WRONG! You need this book! The *Financial Fitness* book is for everyone at any level of wealth. Just like becoming physically or mentally fit, becoming financially fit requires two things: knowing what to do and taking the necessary action to do it. Learn how to prosper, conserve, and become fiscally fantastic. It's a money thing, and the power to prosper is all yours!

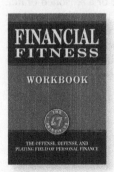

*Financial Fitness Workbook* – $7.95

Economic affairs don't have to be boring or stressful. Make managing money fun in a few simple steps. Use this workbook to get off to a great start and then continue down the right path to becoming fiscally fabulous! Discover exactly where all of your money actually goes as you make note of all your expenditures. Every page will put you one step closer to financial freedom, so purchase the *Financial Fitness Workbook* today and get budgeting!

*Mentoring Matters: Targets, Techniques, and Tools for Becoming a Great Mentor* with Foreword by Orrin Woodward – $19.95

Get your sticky notes ready for all the info you're about to take in from this book. Do you know what it means to be a *great* mentor? It's a key part of successful leadership, but for most people, the necessary skills and techniques don't come naturally. Educate yourself on all of the key targets, techniques, and tools for becoming a magnificent mentor with this easy-to-apply manual. Your leadership success will be forever increased!

**Turn the Page: How to Read Like a Top Leader** with Introduction by Chris Brady – $15.95

Leaders are readers. But there are many ways to read, and leaders read differently than most people do. They read to learn what they need to know, do, or feel, regardless of the author's intent or words. They see past the words and read with the specific intent of finding truth and applying it directly in their own lives. Learn how to read like a top leader so you'll be better able to emulate their success. Applying the skills taught in *Turn the Page* will impact your life, career, and leadership abilities in ways you can't even imagine. So turn the page and start reading!

**SPLASH!: A Leader's Guide to Effective Public Speaking** with Foreword by Chris Brady – $15.95

For many, the fear of giving a speech is worse than the fear of death. But public speaking can be truly enjoyable *and* a powerful tool for making a difference in the lives of others. Whether you are a beginner or a seasoned orator, this book will help you transform your public speaking to a whole new level of leadership influence. Learn the SPLASH formula for great public speaking that will make you the kind of speaker and leader who makes a SPLASH—leaving any audience, big or small, forever changed—every time you speak!

# Subscriptions and Products from
# LIFE Leadership

### The LLR (Launching a Leadership Revolution) Series – $50.00 per month

There is no such thing as a born leader. Based on the *New York Times* bestseller *Launching a Leadership Revolution* by Chris Brady and Orrin Woodward, this series focuses on teaching leadership skills at every level. The principles and specifics taught in the LLR Series will equip you with all the tools you need for business advancement, community influence, church impact, and even an advantage in your home life. Topics include: leadership, finances,  public speaking, goal setting, mentoring, game planning, accountability and tracking of progress, levels of motivation and influence, and leaving a personal legacy. Will you be ready to take the lead when you're called? Subscribe now and learn how to achieve effective confidence skills while growing stronger in your leadership ability.

*Series includes 4 audios and 1 leadership book monthly.*

### The AGO (All Grace Outreach) Series – $25.00 per month

We are all here together to love one another and take care of each other. But sometimes in this hectic world, we lose our way and forget our true purpose. When you subscribe to the AGO Series, you'll gain the valuable support and guidance that every Christian searches for. Nurture your soul, strengthen your faith, and find answers to better understand God's plan for your life, marriage, and children.

*Series includes 1 audio and 1 book monthly.*

### The Edge Series – $10.00 per month

You'll cut in front of the rest of the crowd when you get the *Edge*. Designed for those on the younger side of life, this hard-core, no-frills series promotes self-confidence, drive, and motivation. Get advice, timely information, and true stories of success from interesting talks and fascinating people. Block out the noise around you and learn the principles of self-improvement at an early age. It's a gift that will keep on giving from parent to child. Subscribe today and get a competitive *Edge* on tomorrow.

*Series includes 1 audio monthly.*

### The Freedom Series – $10.00 per month

Freedom must be fought for if it is to be preserved. Every nation and generation needs people who are willing to take a stand for it. Are you one of those brave leaders who'll answer the call? Gain an even greater understanding of the significance and power of freedom, get better informed on issues that affect yours, and find out how you can prevent its decline.

This series covers freedom matters that are important to *you*. Make your freedom and liberty a priority and subscribe today.

*Series includes 1 audio monthly.*

### Financial Fitness Subscription – $10.00 per month for 12 months

If you found the *Financial Fitness Pack* life-changing and beneficial to your bank account, then you'll want even more timely information and guidance from the Financial Fitness Subscription. It's designed as a continuing economic education to help people develop financial discipline and overall knowledge of how their money works. Learn how to make financial principles your financial habits. It's a money thing, and it always pays to be cash savvy.

*Subscription includes 1 audio monthly.*

### LIFE Library Subscription – $40.00 per month

You'll never be shushed in this library. This online, round-the-clock resource is the best connection to LIFE's latest and greatest leadership content. You can watch or listen in either video or audio format, and easy access allows you to search by format, speaker, or subject. Go exploring through the entire content of the LIFE Library. Subscribe today, tune in, and turn it up.

**LIFE Live Subscription – $40.00 per month**
Are you missing out on LIFE? LIFE Live gives you an all-access pass to LIFE Seminars or Webinars all across North America. This cost-effective subscription lets you attend live gatherings in person or by viewing a LIFE Webinar from wherever you are. The LIFE/LLR Session kicks off these live events, which can range in size from a couple hundred to thousands of participants. Now you can continue to keep up with beneficial content and get the latest information you want. Subscribe today. We look forward to seeing you LIVE!

*Financial Fitness Pack* – $99.99
Once and for all, it's time to free yourself from the worry and heavy burden of debt. Decide today to take an honest look at your finances by learning and applying the simple principles of financial success. The *Financial Fitness Pack* provides you with all the tools needed to get on a path to becoming fiscally fantastic!

*Pack includes the* Financial Fitness *book, a companion workbook, and 8 audio recordings.*